COACHING MENTORING AND ASSESSING

COACHING MENTORING AND ASSESSING

a practical guide to developing competence

ERIC PARSLOE

First published in 1992

Reprinted 1993

Kogan Page Limited
120 Pentonville Road
London N1 9JN

British Library Cataloguing in Publication Data
A CIP record for this book is available from the British Library.
ISBN 0 7494 0664 X

Typeset by BookEns Ltd, Baldock, Herts.
Printed in England by Clays Ltd, St Ives plc

Contents

Acknowledgements

I have often wondered why authors want to put acknowledgements at the beginning of their books. I now know why. Without a huge amount of support, effort, encouragement and commitment from a great many people I could not have produced this book in the timescale required. It simply would not have been possible. To say thank you publicly is inadequate but heartfelt.

There are so many to thank that I have organised them into four groups: the people who collaborated on the research in the different organisations; my current colleagues who did the research or provided ideas and support; my other colleagues who helped me gain my knowledge and experience; and finally the small team of support staff who did most of the really hard work finalising the book. In turn I will ask them to pass on my thanks to the people who helped them. So thank you to:

My collaborators: Bruce Fraser, Myra Ashworth and their colleagues in B & Q; John Kenney and his colleagues in Boots the Chemist; Mike Tanner and his colleagues in ICI Pharmaceuticals; Hugh Malkin of Staffordshire Polytechnic Business School for his report published in the Institution of Industrial Managers Manual of Good Practice, Issue No 2, October 1992; Les Ratcliffe and his colleagues in Jaguar Cars; Tony Powell and his colleagues in KPMG Peat Marwick; Sheila Perry of the Management Charter Initiative; Eleanor Bale and her overworked colleagues at the National Council for Vocational Qualifications; Garnet Marshall at the British School of Motoring; Richard Baker at Roussel Laboratories; Kathleen Johnstone and her colleagues at North West Water Ltd; Tricia Campbell; Colin Wilson and his colleagues in Philips Components; Patrick Laryea and their colleagues at the Riverside College of Health Studies; Management Consultants: Sue Edwards, Keith Walton and Kay Williams, and last but not least, Sister Sally Bassett of the Westminster Hospital (who also happens to be my daughter).

My current colleagues: Jim Brathwaite, Stephen Barden, Donald Clark, Andrew 'Toots' Hooley, Carolyn Robertson, Clive Shepherd, Peter Welch, Mike White, Sue Willits and Monika Wray.

My other colleagues: Jan Allen, Joel Cayford, Bridget Farrands, David Hemery, Jan Holmes, David Whitaker and Sir John Whitmore. A special thanks to Granada Computer Services for allowing me, as their Personnel Director, to learn how hard it is to apply ideas in the 'real world'. This is especially true when a business is in trouble and people are primarily concerned with protecting their jobs and careers.

My invaluable support team: Dolores Black for being such a patient editor; Kay Jewell, for organising the production of the manuscript while doing three other jobs simultaneously; Charles Gould, for his skilful researching, writing, handling all the boring details and for his porridge!

Finally, thanks to my own Coach, Mentor and Assessor, my wife, Kay, who has been my sternest critic, staunchest supporter and, at the end thankfully, still my love.

Why Should I Read This Book?

This is a guide book not a theoretical 'instruction' manual. Like all good guide books, it gives directions and suggests routes you might take. I also include recommendations and tips from myself and from other people who have already made these journeys successfully.

I am writing for managers, trainers or consultants who have an interest in knowing more about coaching, mentoring or assessing or any combination of these activities. Your interest may be because you want to become more proficient yourself. Alternatively you may have the responsibility to encourage others you work with to adopt any of these roles. In either case, the outcome you are looking for will be all-round improvement in performance in whatever job is being done in whichever organisation you work for.

My aim is to help you achieve competent performance. A few years ago I might have said my aim was to help you achieve 'excellence'. But recently words like 'excellence', 'competence' and indeed 'quality' have taken on quite different meanings in the context of the world of work. Quality is now often defined as 'fitness for purpose' or put more simply 'meeting the customer's requirements'. This has resulted in excellence or high quality being translated into very specific performance criteria which subsequently can be judged by qualified quality assessors and auditors, as well as by the customer.

Similarly, competent performance can now be defined and assessed against clear performance criteria. These standards may be drawn up by your own organisation to reflect what is needed to produce quality products or services. Often they will have meant the replacement of old appraisal schemes with new performance reviews. Alternatively, these competence standards will lay down the performance that has to be achieved to obtain a professional or vocational qualification. In either case, the achievement of competence is an important objective.

I have assumed that you, the reader, while having a general understanding of coaching, mentoring and assessing are not fully aware of the added dimensions these activities have recently taken on. These new dimensions flow directly from the current 'pursuit of quality and competence'. They also reflect the notion of 'continuous personal improvement' which is part of these philosophies. Coaching and mentoring are concerned with the development of competence. Assessing tends to judge if competence has been achieved. They are, in a sense, two sides of the same coin. All three may be jobs you are asked to do.

I have assumed also that, rather than just read my opinions, you would be interested to learn from the practical experience of others. I have asked people who have been involved in coaching, mentoring or assessing to tell their story. These experiences range from retailing, accountancy, finance, manufacturing, nursing and public services to achieving success in the Olympics and preparing people for their driving tests. Together we point out both the pitfalls to be avoided and the routes to success.

I have structured the book to reflect the practical questions I thought you might ask:

- What do I need to know before I begin?
- What do I have to do if I am asked to be a Coach, Mentor or Assessor?
- What skills do I need to do the job effectively?
- Can you give me more details please?

Each chapter also answers a practical question. I have ended each chapter with an example of 'how to' or a checklist of hints and tips. You don't have to start at the beginning. But it will probably help.

I have always been enthusiastic about new ideas that can contribute to improved performance. I am sure that in one form or another coaching, mentoring and assessing will play a significant part in business success in the next decade. That is why I think it is important for you to read this book. If, when you have finished it, you disagree with me or would like more information, I have included details of how to contact me. I shall look forward to your feedback . . .

Understanding the Language and Jargon

In any specialist subject a private language develops. Below is an alphabetical list which includes definitions of some of the jargon you will find as you begin to learn about the subject of coaching, mentoring and assessing. I also include explanations of abbreviations and acronyms which seem to increase in a never-ending stream of gobbledegook. Although some of the words will already be familiar to many of the readers it is nevertheless well worth reading through the list. Not only will it be a useful reminder but it will also act as an introduction to some of the concepts and definitions we shall be discussing. That is why this section appears at the front of the book.

AAPL
APA
APE
APEL
APL

Vocational qualifications can be acquired by various methods including gaining credit for prior learning, experience, attainment or achievement. Various acronyms are used to describe this process: Attainment, Assessment and Accreditation of Prior Learning. Accreditation of Prior Achievement. Accreditation of Prior Experience. Accreditation of Prior Experience and Learning. The Accreditation of Prior Learning. (Why people can't agree on a single one I really don't know.)

Adviser

The Assessment Adviser is one of the Assessor roles. This person has to be an expert on the assessment process to guide candidates through the competence-based qualification process. The Adviser may be internal to the organisation or external.

Assessor — The Assessor is a specialist who will weigh evidence against the standards and make judgements about competence. There are five assessing roles:
- evaluating performance against an established appraisal or performance review process;
- evaluating performance towards granting an NVQ;
- judging or moderating on behalf of an awarding body;
- managing or verifying the assessment process;
- advising candidates on the process of gaining credit via APL.

Authenticity — Assessors have to be sure that evidence is genuinely the candidate's own work.

C&G — City and Guilds of London Institute is one of the major bodies which award vocational qualifications.

Candidate — I use this term to describe the person undertaking a qualification.

CNAA — Council of National Academic Awards that validates academic qualification at degree level.

Coach — There are four distinct coaching roles:
- 'hands-on', acting as an instructor for inexperienced learners;
- 'hands-off', developing high performance in experienced learners;
- 'supporter', when helping learners use a flexible learning package;
- 'qualifier', when helping a learner develop a specific requirement for a competence-based or professional qualification.

Competence — The ability to perform in the workplace to the standards expected by employers and which are nationally agreed.

Counsellor — Sometimes used to describe a Mentor.

Credit — A credit is gained on achievement of one unit of competence towards a full national vocational qualification.

Development plan I use this term to describe a written plan. It is similar to either a learning plan or a learning contract. This action plan defines the general goals and objectives for a range of development activities to be completed within a set timescale. The plan should be signed off by the learner and the other people involved.

Diary/work logs Records of daily activities and events which will contribute towards a portfolio of evidence.

Element of competence Units of competence are subdivided into separate elements which define what a competent person is expected to be able to perform in specific aspects of their work role.

Evidence of competence Evidence is required to support all claims to competence in specific units or elements. It can take several forms including observation of work being performed or documents produced by the candidate (direct evidence) and/or information about the candidate such as statements from employers/customers/suppliers (indirect evidence).

ILB Industry Lead Body, an organisation established by the government, which has the responsibility for coordinating the agreement of standards of performance for a specific industry.

Learner I use this term to describe someone who is learning to improve their performance by working with a Coach or by some other method.

Learning contract A written agreement between a learner and a manager or Coach on behalf of an organisation defining learning goals, methods and timescales.

MCI The Management Charter Initiative; an organisation which was created to produce performance standards for the role of managers. It has acted as an Industry Lead Body in this respect.

Mentor A wise and trusted counsellor but with three distinct mentoring roles in the work context:

- the mainstream mentor; someone who acts as a guide, adviser and counsellor at various stages in someone's career from induction through formal development to a top management position;
- the professional qualification mentor; someone required by a professional association to be appointed to guide a student through a programme of study, leading to a professional qualification;
- the vocational qualification mentor; someone appointed to guide a candidate through a programme of development and the accumulation and presentation of evidence to prove competence to a standard required for a National Vocational Qualification.

NCVQ National Council for Vocational Qualifications which oversees and validates all vocational qualifications.

NVQs National Vocational Qualifications. These are qualifications awarded by various bodies authorised by the NCVQ. They are divided into different levels:

LEVEL 1: for competence in basic tasks and functions which are routine and require little responsibility or autonomy. They are mainly performed with strong support and guidance.

LEVEL 2: for competence in complex but still routine activities. A certain degree of autonomy is expected.

LEVEL 3: for competence in a broad range of activities, most of which are complex and non-routine. There is considerable responsibility and autonomy, and control or guidance of others is often required.

LEVEL 4: for competence in complex, technical or professional work activities with a substantial degree of personal responsibility and autonomy. Responsibility for the work of others and the allocation of resources is often present.

	LEVEL 5: for competence at a higher level. Very little work has yet been done but from 1993 onwards these qualifications will increasingly exist.
Performance criteria	Clearly define the expected level of performance for every element in an NVQ unit of competence.
Performance profile	A breakdown of established performance abilities a candidate has in relation to specific elements of competence.
Personal competence	The personal qualities, skills and attributes associated with effective working behaviour.
Personal report	A report (usually written) describing actions and functions carried out, presented as evidence in relation to specific elements of competence.
Portfolio	The file in which all the necessary information and evidence of competence is presented for assessment.
Protégé	I use this term for an inexperienced person (usually young) who is assigned to a Mentor. I certainly prefer this term to 'Mentee' which some people use.
Qualification	Completing all the units will result in a nationally recognised qualification from awarding bodies such as BTEC, City and Guilds, CNAA, RSA or from a professional body.
RSA	The Royal Society of Arts – a major awarding body of vocational qualifications.
Range statements	These are statements of the range of circumstances to which an element of competence applies and for which evidence of competent performance must be produced.
Regional Verification Panel	A mechanism for quality assurance through verification of assessments usually by a group of expert Assessors and representatives of an awarding body.
SCOTVEC	Is the Scottish Vocational Verification Council and is the Scottish equivalent of the NCVQ.
SVQ	Scottish Vocational Qualification, issued by

	SCOTVEC in a similar way to NCVQ.
Transferability	The demonstrable ability to perform a function competently in various contexts or situations.
Underpinning knowledge	The body of knowledge and technical information a candidate needs to perform a task competently.
Unit of competence	Each set of standards is subdivided into a number of units of competence which describe in broad terms what is expected of someone in their job role.
Verification	A quality assurance process to confirm and monitor that consistent assessments are being made.

CHAPTER 1
How Do Adults Learn?

Developing competence is about learning. Whether you are a Coach, Mentor or Assessor, you need to understand the basics of how adults learn if you are to help them at all.

Most adults at some time in their lives have probably tried to learn how to drive a car. Let's see how they go about it and compare each approach with what happens at work. Some take their first step by reading books about it. They buy the *Highway Code* and the Ministry of Transport manual *Driving*. They pick up a lot of information this way but they are certainly not ready to go on the road and drive.

People also learn to do their job through reading textbooks and studying theories about how people behave at work. This may be a good way for them to start. It can give them an intellectual understanding so that they have the confidence to start learning the skills. The danger is that theories on their own can get in the way when people are faced with the complicated, muddled reality of doing the job at work.

Another way of learning to drive is to borrow a car and crawl around a field or deserted car park on a Sunday morning. You can stall and crash the gears and generally learn from your mistakes. No one is at risk. However, it can sometimes be difficult to transfer what you've learned to a busy road.

Learning to do your job through trial and error is the basis of many training programmes. Some people enjoy the activities on such courses. People usually do learn best when they are having fun. But without some intellectual learning to go with it, it can sometimes be time consuming and does not always produce obvious improvements in their skills.

A third way of learning to drive that people choose is to sit in the passenger seat and watch the driver. There is no pressure on the learner and a lot can be picked up. But the person being watched may not be an ideal example: they may have some bad habits they are unaware of that will not impress the examiner when the learner copies them in the test.

'Sitting by Nelly' is one of the most common ways used to transfer a technical skill: 'Watch how I do it and then copy me.' People also learn to be managers through watching how they themselves are managed. This may not be a deliberate piece of learning but we are all influenced to some extent by the way our managers manage us and the way we see them being managed. This is how people learn the 'management style' of an organisation.

Then there is the 'in at the deep end' approach. You get your learner's licence and simply jump in the car and drive. It's the first time ever; you stall at the traffic lights, ignore everyone blowing their horns and terrify a pedestrian by not noticing them crossing . . . But you are driving. It's demanding, certainly exciting and never boring. But it can be terrifying to watch and unnecessarily dangerous.

'Sink or swim' is a common way of learning how to do your job. For some people it's the only way. The pressure of having to do it is so powerful it forces them to learn very quickly. For others it can be a disaster. Their confidence can be so damaged they become convinced they haven't 'got what it takes'. The result may not be 'survival of the fittest' so much as the survival of a particular kind of learner. In at the deep end may mean some good people get drowned before they have a chance to swim.

Of course, one of the most effective ways of learning to drive is to pay a trained instructor to coach you through the test. The best driving schools have cars with dual controls so that the instructor can start with hands and feet firmly on the controls. As your experience increases, and the instructor's confidence grows, they can increasingly let go of the controls. We shall return to this 'hands-on–hands-off' approach to coaching later.

Learning to learn

Learning can be more effective if people can be allowed, or taught, to use more than one way of learning. The trainer's jargon for this is 'to use one or more learning strategies'. A popular strategy is to use 'mind maps' which are the brainchild of Tony Buzan. A mind map is a visual memory aid. The aim is to create a whole network of notes and ideas on a sheet of paper, starting at the centre with the main concept, then branching out using key words and images. Some people find it much easier to remember things when they can picture them in their mind's eye. The mind map works on this principle so that the more striking and imaginative it is, the more likely it is, Buzan advocates, that you will be able to remember it clearly (see Figure 1.1). At a simpler level, people use acronyms and other techniques, to help them memorise certain key pieces of information.

Experience has taught me also that different people, if they are given the choice, prefer to learn in different ways. Everyone has their own preferred learning styles, different starting points for the learning process. Thinking about learning as a process is another way of looking at how people learn. How often have you heard 'You're never too old to learn' or in a sporting situation 'she won the next set by calling on her experience to outwit the younger player'? Learning from experience can be seen as a continuous process or cycle.

The starting point in the cycle is to experience something. It could be a presentation, demonstration or an incident during normal work. After the event, inevitably and perhaps subconsciously, comes a period of reflection or thinking about what happened. This leads you to draw certain conclusions for yourself. In turn you then have to decide what you would do if you experience a similar event in future. You plan to do this and put it into practice the next time. Depending on what happens, you may go through the whole process again and again and again. Hopefully, each time the need to modify future activity becomes less, as you become more 'experienced'. But the process need never stop altogether.

That is the theory. The reality is that a lot of people simply 'switch off' and ignore the learning process. This may be because they see no point or reward in it or have no opportunity to learn and develop in new ways. For many, however, the boredom or day-to-day pressures in a job discourage them from thinking about learning. Many also have the erroneous attitude that learning means training courses, and unless you are sent on a course you can't be learning. But even for those who don't share these attitudes and are motivated to learn, it is important they understand that it is a continuous process. This means there are lots of opportunities but it takes time. 'Practice makes perfect' may be an irritating proverb for the impatient learner. But it contains an important truth.

FIG 1.1 MIND MAP

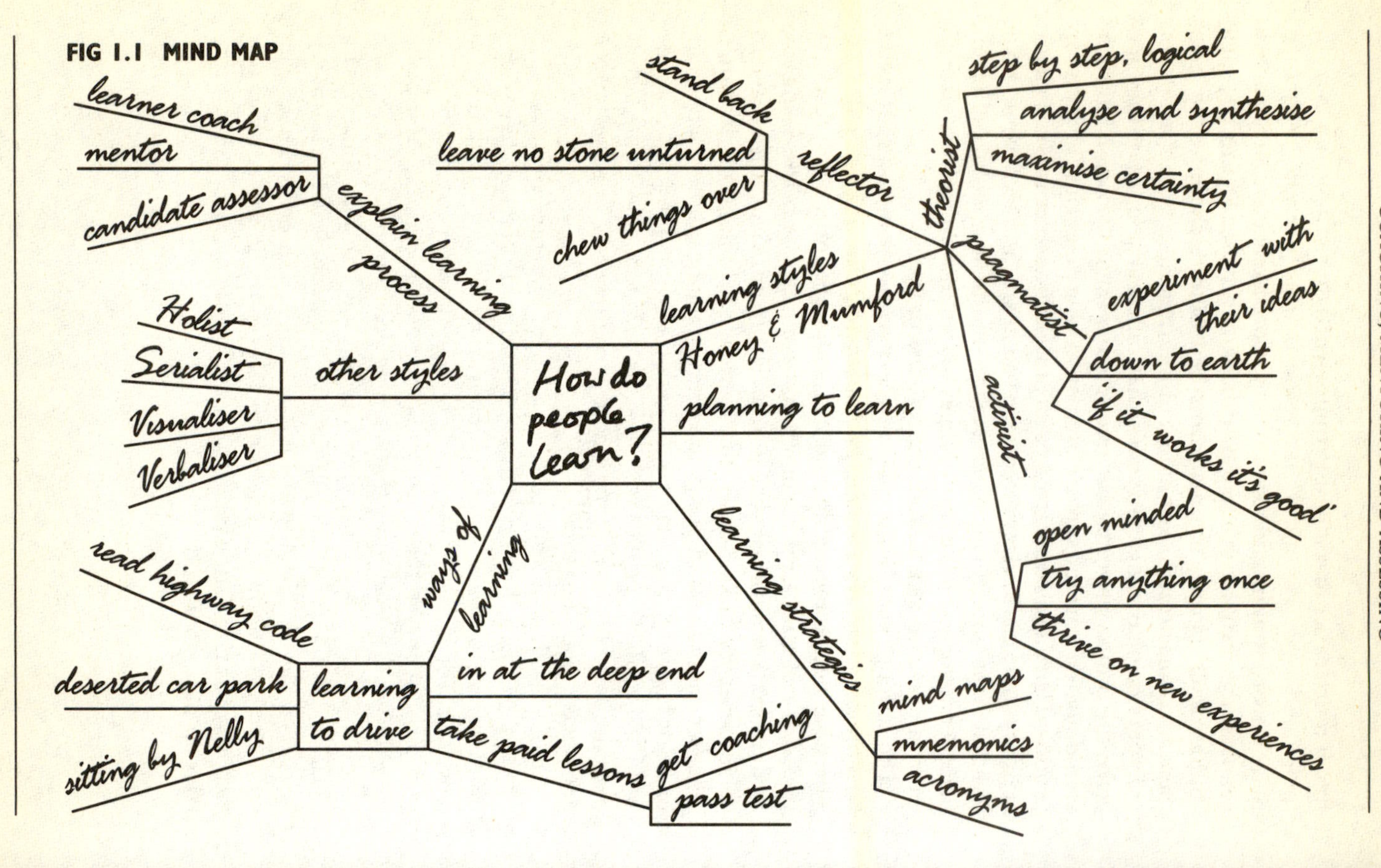

Learning styles

The Coach, Mentor and Assessor have to understand and be able to explain the learning process. They should be able also to recognise their learner's, protégé's or candidate's preferred learning style. Some styles conflict strongly with others. Some people prefer to see the big picture first before they begin. They are termed 'holists' because they take a holistic view. Others prefer to work step by logical step and build up the big picture. They are termed 'serialists'. Some are happier when new ideas are presented visually; others prefer to listen, talk and discuss. These are termed 'visualisers' and 'verbalisers'. The responsibility for adjusting styles to provide the maximum help in the most effective way lies with the Coach, Mentor or Assessor. To do this, they must first be clear about their own preference.

Among the most influential thinkers and writers on the topic of learning styles have been Peter Honey and Alan Mumford. Their work has been based on a respectable body of research and their conclusion and ideas have become familiar parts of many training programmes. A typical summary of their four main learning styles is being used by Mike Tanner, the Flexible Learning Manager for ICI Pharmaceuticals, for his own learners' guidance.

'**Activists** Activists involve themselves fully and without bias in new experiences. They enjoy the here and now and are happy to be dominated by immediate experiences. They are open-minded, not sceptical, and this tends to make them enthusiastic about anything new. Their philosophy is: "I'll try anything once". They tend to throw caution to the wind. Their days are filled with activity. They revel in short-term crisis fire-fighting. They tackle problems by brainstorming. As soon as the excitement from one activity has died down they are busy looking for the next. They tend to thrive on the challenge of new experiences but are bored with implementation and longer-term consolidation. They are gregarious people constantly involving themselves with others but, in doing so, they hog the limelight. They are the life and soul of the party and seek to centre all activities around themselves.

Reflectors Reflectors like to stand back to ponder experiences and observe them from many different perspectives. They collect data, both first hand and from others, and prefer to chew it over thoroughly before coming to any conclusion. The thorough collection and analysis of data about experiences and events is what counts, so they tend to postpone reaching definitive conclusions for as long as possible. Their philosophy is to be cautious, to leave no stone unturned. They are thoughtful people who like to consider all possible angles and implications before making a move. They prefer to take a back seat in meetings and discussions. They enjoy observing other people in action. They listen to others and get the drift of the discussion before making their own points. They tend to adopt a low profile and have a slightly distant, tolerant, unruffled air about them. When they act it is a part of a wider picture which includes the past as well as the present and the observations of others as well as their own.

Theorists Theorists adapt and integrate observations into complex but logically sound theories. They think problems through in a vertical, step-by-step logical way. They assimilate disparate facts into coherent theories. They tend to be perfectionists who won't rest easy until things are tidy and fit into their rational scheme. They like to analyse and synthesise. They are keen on basic assumptions, principles, theories, models and systems thinking. Their philosophy prizes rationality and logic: "If it's logical, it's good." Questions they frequently ask are: "Does it make sense?"; "How does it fit with that?"; "What are the basic assumptions?" They tend to be detached, analytical, and dedicated to rational objectivity rather than anything subjective or ambiguous. Their approach to problems is consistently logical. This is their "mental set" and they rigidly reject anything that doesn't fit with it. They prefer to maximise certainty and feel uncomfortable with subjective judgements, lateral thinking, and anything flippant.

Pragmatists Pragmatists are keen on trying out ideas, theories, and techniques to see if they work in practice. They actively search out new ideas and take the first opportunity to experiment with applications. They are the sort of people who return from management courses brimming with new ideas that they want to try out in practice. They like to get on with things and act quickly and confidently on ideas that attract them. They don't like beating about the bush and tend to be impatient with ruminating and open-ended discussions. They are essentially practical, down-to-earth people who like making practical decisions and solving problems. They respond to problems and opportunities as a challenge. Their philosophy is: "There is always a better way", and "If it *works* it's good".'

Honey and Mumford have developed a questionnaire technique which allows you to identify how strongly you prefer each of their styles (see Appendix 1, p 154) They advocate that people will learn more effectively if they can choose learning opportunities to suit their strongest preferences. This may not be just one style but perhaps a combination of two or three, but with, maybe, a strong dislike for one particular style. They do not claim that people cannot learn from situations which do not suit their preference. Indeed they suggest ways that you can develop your less preferred styles to enable you to maximise your learning opportunities.

Interestingly, their research suggests that people in certain types of jobs have tendencies to preferred styles as follows:

- *Salesmen* Stronger preferences towards pragmatist and activist.
- *Trainers* Slightly stronger preference towards reflector and pragmatist.
- *Marketing managers* Higher preference towards reflector and pragmatist, and low preference towards activist.
- *Engineering/science graduates* High preference towards reflectors; much lower towards activist.
- *Research & Development managers* Similar but even sharper preferences and dislikes than Engineering/Science graduates.
- *Production managers* Very high preference towards pragmatist and theorist, and very low towards activist.
- *Finance managers* Strong preferences towards pragmatist, reflector and theorist, and lower towards activist than any of the other types of jobholders.

Planning to learn

Understanding, and being able to explain, how different people learn is essential if you are to guide people towards their most effective development route. Armed with this understanding, you should be able also to recognise that your own preferences may not suit someone else. If you start off your relationship with a learner with a thorough analysis and discussion of these issues, obvious pitfalls can be avoided. More importantly, as a result of this type of discussion you can help the learner to plan their learning and development.

Drawing up a development plan should not be seen as an academic exercise or quick fix before you rush into action. To achieve tangible development or vocational qualifications you will need the active and positive support of people you work with. You are more likely to gain this support if you can show a clear and realistic plan. Indeed in many organisations, the development plan or 'learning contract', where both the learner and the manager 'sign-off' the proposed development programme, has become a recognised method of formalising the commitment to each other.

How to produce a development plan

There are four stages to producing a development plan:

1. Assess current performance and skills.
2. Prioritise needs.
3. Choose appropriate development methods.
4. Present plan for 'sign-off'.

Planning is always made easier if suitable documents are available; you should avoid planning on the back of a cigarette packet! To illustrate the process and the type of forms you need, follow the forms in the diagrams given later in the chapter. You will see that we have used coaching as an example as it seems appropriate.

Stage One is to assess your current performance using a profiling technique (see Figure 1.2). Start by assessing yourself against each performance standard using a scale of good, average or weak. Answer honestly as there is no point in kidding yourself. Not every element may apply to your situation so you need to indicate that whenever it is appropriate. Equally important is the need to indicate if you don't know or don't understand the requirement. In either case, it should tell you that it is a high priority for you to learn at least the basics.

Your own assessment should be accompanied by your manager's views and those of at least one colleague, who may be another Coach or someone who you have coached. It is important to test your own views against other people's so ask them to do it independently and equally frankly. You then need to do the same exercise on the skills profile (see Figure 1.3).

Stage Two is to combine each of your assessments on to a development planner (see Figure 1.4). This allows you to judge which topics are a high, medium or low priority for you to learn. You can then match these priorities with your own learning style preferences and the learning opportunities available. Don't rely entirely on your own ideas. Discuss the options with your Coach, Mentor, manager or colleagues as they may point you towards learning opportunities that had not occurred to you. If the opportunities available do not suit your own learning preferences, you have two choices. Either you discuss with your Coach, Mentor or manager what other routes you could take or you recognise in advance that you need to improve your learning abilities in styles that you don't really like.

The third stage is to transfer your conclusions on priority topics and appropriate methods to your development plan (see Figure 1.5). You will realise that you are asked to commit to a start and completion date. Don't make rash decisions. Think carefully about the implications and resolve to meet the dates you set yourself. This is particularly important because you are encouraged to get your plan 'signed-off' by your Coach and manager. This should be a two-way commitment. You, having set your own topics, methods and timescale, are asking for time and support from others to help you achieve your plan. The more realistic you have been, the more likely you are to receive a positive response.

FIG 1.2 COACHING PERFORMANCE PROFILE

No.	PERFORMANCE STANDARD	1	2	3	N/A	D/KU
	ANALYSE					
1	Assess current standards of performance					
2	Identify learning needs to meet performance goals and required standards					
	PLAN					
3	Identify and organise suitable learning resource(s) and opportunities					
4	Agree learning plans, coaching role and assessment methods					
5	Provide opportunities for individuals and groups to manage their own learning					
6	Agree and organise the appropriate level of support to the learner					
7	Organise facilitation of workshops and action learning groups as appropriate					
	IMPLEMENT					
8	Explain, demonstrate and supervise practice of concepts and techniques					
9	Ensure opportunities for feedback and discussion					
10	Adjust coaching role and programme to suit learner's needs and progress					
11	Explain how flexible packages can be used to good effect					
12	Demonstrate the use of any technology involved					
13	Explain clearly the standards and performance criteria required for the qualification required					
14	Liaise effectively with other people supporting the candidate's qualification programme					
15	Demonstrate awareness of Health and Safety, Equal Opportunities, Employment Law and Special Needs issues					
	EVALUATE					
16	Evaluate achievement of goals and standards					
17	Provide feedback, encouragement and support to individuals to apply learning					
18	Enable the candidate to collect and present appropriate evidence for assessment					

Please assess using the following ratings:

1 Good
2 Average
3 Weak
N/A Not applicable
D/KU Don't know or don't understand

Once you have completed the ratings enter them on the Development Planner

Assessment check list	✓
Self	
Line-Manager	
Colleague	

FIG 1.3 COACHING SKILLS PROFILE

No.	SKILLS STANDARD	1	2	3	N/A	D/KU
1	Listen attentively					
2	Observe and recognise competent performance					
3	Demonstrate effective questioning technique					
4	Respond, summarise and clarify situations					
5	Recognise different learning styles					
6	Adapt to preferred learning styles					
7	Adopt appropriate coaching styles					
8	Gain acceptance and commitment to performance goals from learner					
9	Display sensitivity to and empathy for learners' thoughts and ideas and need for appropriate feedback					
10	Establish rapport and good communication channels with learner					
11	Encourage learner to take responsibility for own development					
12	Support and build confidence in learner					
13	Lead and facilitate workshops and action learning groups					
14	Build good working relationships with team members in various parts of the organisation					
15						
16						
17						
18						
19						
20						

Please assess using the following ratings:

- **1** Good
- **2** Average
- **3** Weak
- **N/A** Not applicable
- **D/KU** Don't know or don't understand

Once you have completed the ratings enter them on the Development Planner

Assessment check list

	✓
Self	
Line-Manager	
Colleague	

FIG 1.4 DEVELOPMENT PLANNER

No.	PERFORMANCE RATING				Action	ACTION REQUIRED
	Self	Manager	Colleague	Colleague	Priority	
1						
2						
3						
4						
5						
6						
7						
8						
9						
10						
11						
12						
13						
14						
15						
16						
17						
18						
19						
20						

Once you have obtained ratings from yourself, your line-manager and at least one colleague, enter the scores here. Then decide the priority for action using the following ratings:

ACTION PRIORITY

H = High

M = Medium

L = Low

Use the planner to match your priorities and learning preferences with the opportunities available. Transfer this information to your learning plan.

Please assess using the following ratings:

1 Good
2 Average
3 Weak
N/A Not applicable
D/KU Don't know or don't under-stand

FIG 1.5 DEVELOPMENT PLAN

TOPIC: ______

	Start Date	Complete by
Book		
Discs		
Assignments		
Projects		

TOPIC: ______

	Start Date	Complete by
Book		
Discs		
Assignments		
Projects		

TOPIC: ______

	Start Date	Complete by
Book		
Discs		
Assignments		
Projects		

TOPIC: ______

	Start Date	Complete by
Book		
Discs		
Assignments		
Projects		

TOPIC: ______

	Start Date	Complete by
Book		
Discs		
Assignments		
Projects		

SIGN OFF

	Learner	Coach/Manager
Signed		
Title		
Date		

TOPIC: ______

	Start Date	Complete by
Book		
Discs		
Assignments		
Projects		

TOPIC: ______

	Start Date	Complete by
Book		
Discs		
Assignments		
Projects		

INSTRUCTIONS

For each topic fill in the start date for any of the activities you will use during your development. Then commit to a date for each activity to be completed by. You should get the plan for this signed off by your manager and/or coach before you begin. The plan will be the basis for regular review sessions.

CHAPTER 2
How Do People Become Qualified?

The appetite to become qualified seems to be a permanent feature of people brought up in our society, and appears to remain constant across generations. I can remember, as a child, the constant pressure to 'do well at school' so that I could go first to grammar school and then possibly to university. Obtaining a degree, my father thought, was a passport to joining the governing and administrative elite. If I failed at school, I would have to remain in the 'labouring class'. But here too qualifications were important if I could get a trade with an apprenticeship.

This early conditioning is undoubtedly still going on, although the language and ideas have changed. Words like pass and fail, elite and class, have been a feature of British society and therefore of education and training also, for most of the twentieth century. The debate about the institutions and processes that accompany them has been fierce. Over the past 20 years the pendulum has swung from the ascendancy of liberal comprehensive ideas back towards the conservative and elitist approach. But, by the 1990s, a surprising consensus seems to have begun to emerge between employers, employees, politicians and academics that a coherent structure of qualifications and a more realistic open access and development path towards gaining them is an important national priority.

Four basic ideas accepted

The simple idea that the curriculum taught in the schools, colleges and universities should relate closely to the needs of every occupation that people might subsequently follow in their working lives has been widely accepted, albeit somewhat reluctantly by some academics. So too has the idea that people's needs and desires to gain access to education and training might change during their lives. Consequently, the providers of education and training need to plan highly flexible and varied opportunities for people with widely different needs and abilities.

Two other ideas underpin what can reasonably be called a revolution in our national thinking about education and training which has happened without most people being aware that it was taking place. The first is that, instead of most qualifications being dominated by the 'final examination pass or fail' approach, they should in future be based primarily on assessment of what people can demonstrate they can do competently. The second idea is that people should be able to obtain these competence-based qualifications by producing evidence of competence by whichever method is appropriate, including that of gaining credits from prior experience.

It is of course true that the debate continues fiercely about the details and the serious implications of the implementation of these ideas. There are enthusiastic purists and pragmatists on each issue as in any debate. But to my mind grasping that these simple ideas will be implemented is the secret to understanding how you may gain qualifications in the future.

Convergence of academic and vocational qualifications

One of the main thinkers behind the 'qualification revolution' has been Gilbert Jessup who at the time of writing is Deputy Chief Executive of the National Council for Vocational Qualifications (NCVQ). He outlines most of the issues in the debate in his book *Outcome: NVQs and the emerging model of education and training*. He uses the diagram shown in Figure 2.1 to illustrate his model. From the base of the National Education Curriculum, students can progress through a route of A-levels and degrees or an equivalent parallel route of National Vocational Qualifications (NVQs) with various levels of qualifications from 1 to 5. Overlapping these routes are core skills which are relevant to both types of qualification and which are soon to be recognised by an additional general NVQ qualification.

The intention is that, as the decade progresses, the academic and vocational qualification processes will converge; both in practice and

FIG 2.1 A FRAMEWORK FOR EDUCATION AND TRAINING

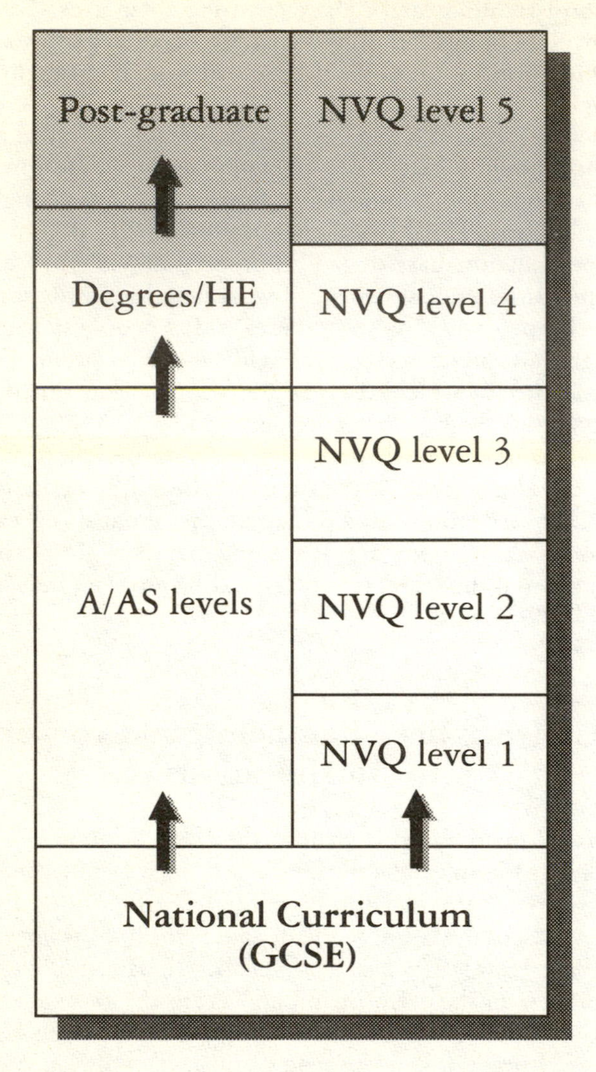

eventually in acceptance in people's minds. To understand that this process will not be simple, one only has to consider the jungle of current qualification providers. It is estimated that there are more then 80 business schools, more than 120 professional institutes or associations, hundreds and hundreds of colleges of further and higher education and polytechnics. All of them can provide access to awards from several different awarding bodies such as City and Guilds, RSA and BTEC. Then too there are an increasing number of universities which grant their own awards.

Winning agreement from all these vested interests to adopt a coherent strategy is clearly a nightmare task. But considerable progress has been made and the target for having an NVQ available to 80 per cent of the workforce in Britain by the end of 1992 could well have been achieved. But having a qualification available is one thing. Having people obtain the qualifications and, subsequently having the qualifications accepted, is another. Time will tell. Obviously current practice will continue in some occupations and professions almost unchanged for a considerable time. But for many people who have previously not had access to qualifications, the changes have already happened as I explain in Chapter 6.

Examination versus assessment

There are important differences between the historic academic examination type of qualification and the competence-based qualification. To help understand these differences, two pieces of jargon need to be simplified. Academic qualifications have usually been 'norm-referenced' and competence-based qualifications are mainly 'criterion-referenced'. Norm-referenced means that the examiners accept that there is a normal distribution of ability in any population of students seeking the qualification. It is possible therefore to set exams which will test knowledge and understanding in such a way that those with the highest knowledge and understanding will score the highest marks and vice versa. And because ability is always distributed normally, you can set pass or fail marks and a scale of grades or classification of ability. Critics of these systems have argued that, while it produces accurate measures of relative levels of knowledge on a set day, that result is not necessarily a useful guide to future performance of tasks or skills. It is also a system which is consciously designed to classify quite a high proportion of students as failures, with nothing to show for their efforts.

Criterion-referenced, on the other hand, means that the qualification is based on clear statements of desired outcomes, each with detailed performance criteria which, if attained, leave no doubt as to the achievement of a candidate. As qualification levels can be carefully designed in advance, many more candidates end up successfully completing a process that clearly defines their competence. Critics argue that defining the criteria for all subjects, tasks and skills is an almost impossible task and that the approach gives no indication of the relative abilities of a candidate but merely measures the lowest common acceptable denominator. Inevitably there are strengths and weaknesses in both approaches and situations where one is more appropriate than the other. The early advocates of competence-based, criterion-referenced qualifications have had to accept that, while it is superior for many functions and possibly for some skills, in the area of testing knowledge and understanding it is probably weaker. Combining the two approaches, whenever possible and appropriate, clearly makes sense - but also complicates the administration!

The basic NVQ structure

When you look at National Vocational Qualifications for any occupation, you will find they have similar structures. All are divided into levels. The first level will be for basic functions which are routine and require little responsibility or autonomy. They are mainly performed with strong support and guidance from a supervisor or manager. As the degree of complexity and responsibility increases and as more supervisory or management functions are required so the level of qualification rises. Level 5 will be the highest level and will have a similar status to a higher or post-graduate academic degree.

The second feature is that the NVQ is divided into key roles each of which cover a distinct aspect of an occupation, eg for a manager, the key roles are: managing operations, managing finance, managing people and managing information. Each key role is then divided into distinct units and each unit sub-divided into elements. Each element has its own set of clear performance criteria. The structure is illustrated in Figure 2.2.

Each element also has a statement of the range of situations that a candidate at that level must be able to apply the performance to. This is intended to ensure that the function performed can be transferred with equal competence from one situation to another. Each element also has a statement of the level of knowledge to be tested to show the required understanding of how and why the function is being performed. This part of the process is important as knowledge underpins the competent execution of the function. As the level of the responsibility and autonomy rises, there is also, for each element, an increasingly

FIG 2.2 NVQ STATEMENT OF COMPETENCE

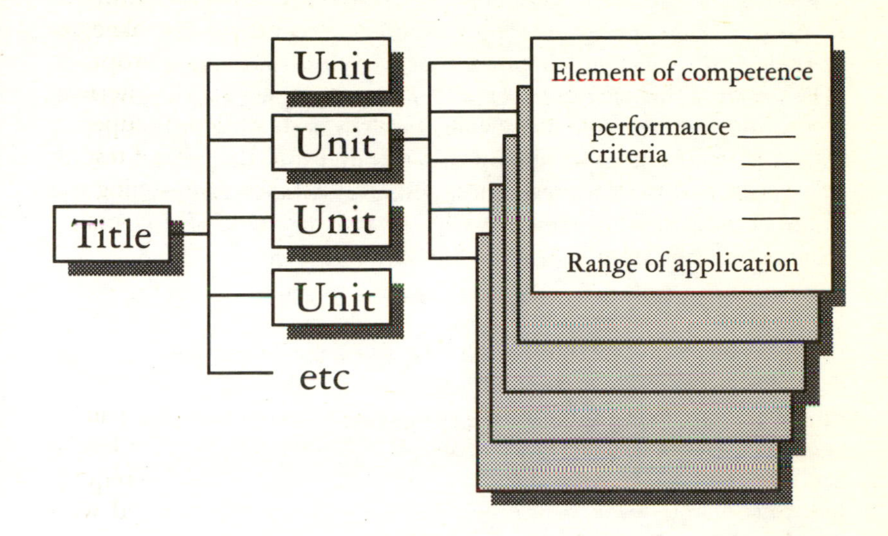

demanding statement of the personal or core skills that should be demonstrated and tested in meeting the competent performance of the function.

As its critics point out, this makes for a very complicated situation for the candidate and the Assessor to cope with. But its advocates claim that the system produces better results and its initial complexity will soon become understood and accepted.

NVQs for everyone?

To establish qualifications for every occupation, the government established Industry Lead Bodies (ILBs). These bodies were made up of the employers and leading professional, academic and operational organisations within the industry. Their function has been to draw up the full NVQ specification for occupations in their industry. Similarly the Management Charter Initiative (MCI) was formed to define NVQs for management which is a job that crosses most industries. Most ILBs started with the basic jobs because it was these that often had fewer current qualifications available. And, equally important, because the higher up the occupational hierarchy you go the stronger the vested interests are and the longer it takes to gain agreement to change.

As the NVQ system 'rolls out', more and more people will have access to the qualifications. These qualifications can be built up one unit at a time and in an order that suits the individual's current requirements and preferences. Employers in future therefore will increasingly be presented with Records of Achievement (or Attainment). This may resemble a chessboard of Units that the candidate for a job or promotion obtained here, there and everywhere. Figure 2.3 illustrates this concept. Increasingly, these Records will be held on a national register and it is not too fanciful to envisage situations where competence-based qualifications become a requirement for people to be licensed to perform in occupations like plumbing, for instance. If this happens, it will be another illustration of the convergence of practices with our colleagues from other European countries. The European dimension is, of course, another factor which has given impetus to the changes which are occurring.

How quickly will NVQs be adopted?

Recognising the strengths and weaknesses of Records of Achievement will be the least of new burdens employers will have to face. Fundamental to the concept of vocational qualifications is that they need to be assessed in the workplace. Only there it is argued can genuinely competent performance usually be observed. A whole army of workplace Assessors will be needed. This involves understanding the assessment process (see Figure 2.4). Also a massive training programme will be needed. More detailed involvement will also be necessary with the education and training institutions who have historically carried out most of these development and awarding activities on behalf of the industry.

The Accreditation of Prior Learning (APL) or Accreditation of Prior Achievement (APA) process in particular, allows people greater flexibility on how to collect the evidence to prove their competence. This greater flexibility poses some awkward problems. Education and training organisations will have to adjust their programmes to become more modular. Teaching staff will have to adapt to new student requirements. Awarding bodies will have to ensure that their Assessors are properly trained and equipped to cope with the APL process. Not

FIG 2.3 THE NVQ FRAMEWORK

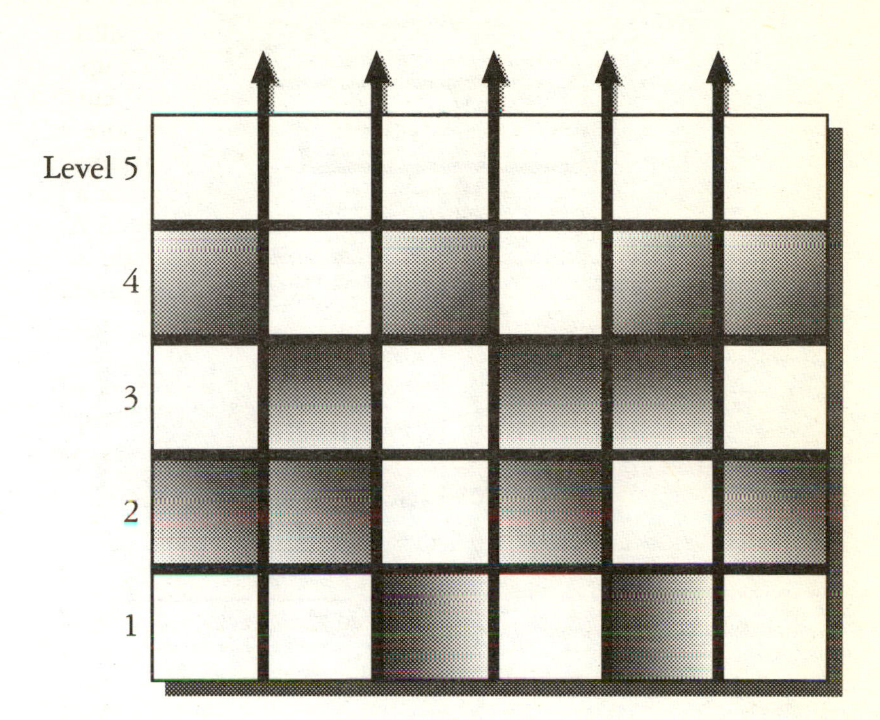

least the candidates will need help and support to negotiate their way through the new system. A new role – the Assessment Adviser – will be needed to help everyone concerned, including Coaches, Mentors and Assessors.

The end result of this new and additional activity, supporters claim, will be a substantial and significant improvement in the all-round competent performance from all occupations in the economy. I accept this as a desirable objective; but, like many other people, I have found the size, complexity and implications of these changes difficult to understand, let alone plan to implement. This complexity when added to the economics of business and the inherent reluctance to accept these types of change, must pose a question on the speed with which these new qualifications will be adopted in practice rather than

FIG 2.4 THE ASSESSMENT PROCESS

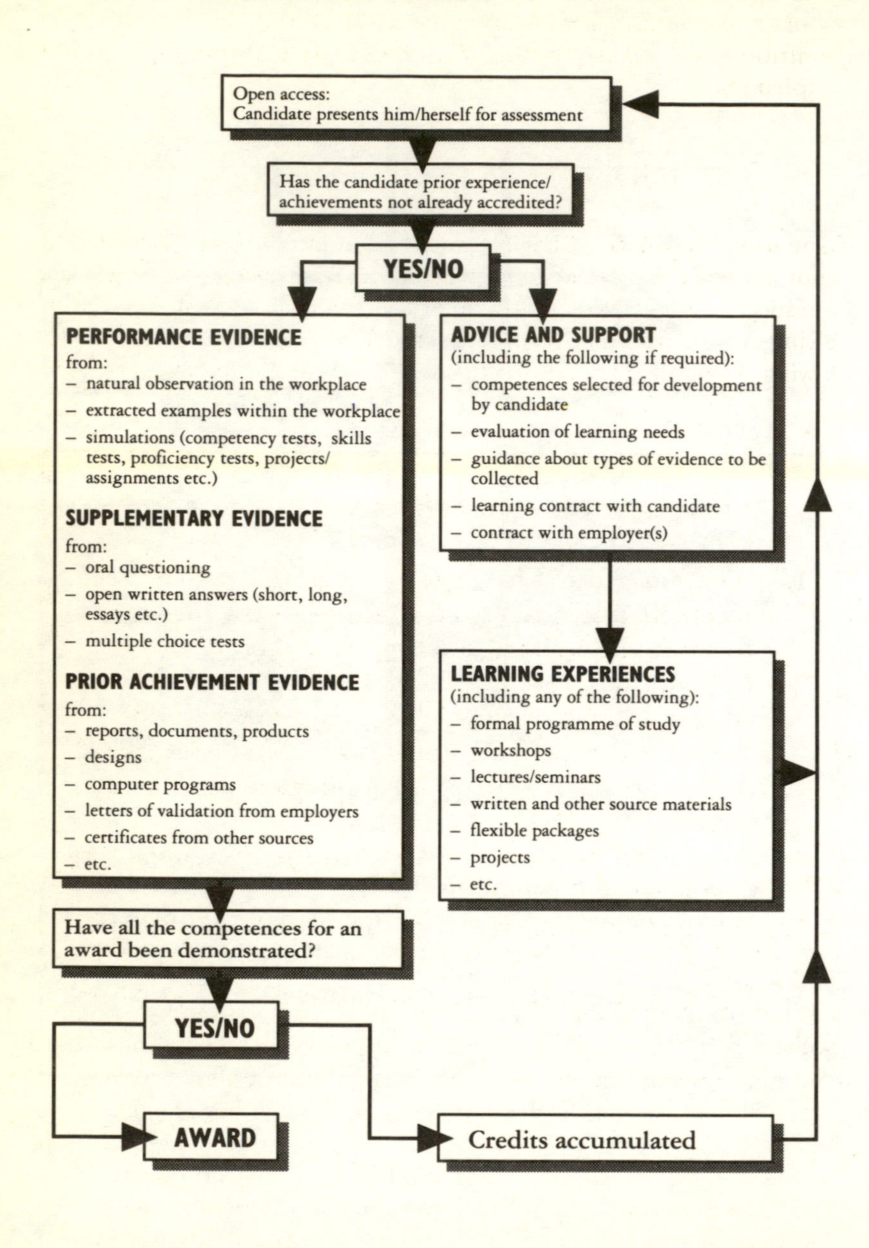

with lip service. Incomprehension can be overcome of course. This book, and the associated training package, are in part intended as a contribution to making it easier for other people to comprehend and implement.

Checking your understanding

One useful technique I have learned to adopt is always to check that your audience has understood your message by asking them a few key questions. This is particularly helpful if the message you have been giving is as complicated as in this chapter. So: can you answer the following questions confidently. If not, try re-reading the chapter.

Checklist

1. What are the four basic ideas that have been accepted which have led to the changes in the way vocational qualifications will be awarded?
2. Can you describe how students can progress from education up the vocational qualification ladder?
3. What are the main advantages and disadvantages of qualifications based on exams rather than assessment?
4. How is an NVQ divided into units, elements and performance criteria?
5. What are Industry Lead Bodies and how does MCI fit in?
6. What is the APL or APA process designed to achieve?

CHAPTER 3
What is Evidence of Competence?

Candidates for National Vocational Qualifications no longer have to sit exams, but they do have to prove they are competent. Anyone who needs to prove a case needs evidence. The most obvious example is that of a prosecuting or defending lawyer who needs to show evidence to prove the guilt or innocence of their client.

Evidence can be first hand and direct as when the defendant makes his own case from the witness stand. Or it can be indirect evidence from others about the defendant. This is evidence which confirms the defendant's own story or alibi or it can be the evidence of responsible people who offer character references confirming the defendant is a law-abiding and honourable person. The direct evidence may often be stronger, but a combination of both is usually required to be convincing.

Evidence presented in the courtroom can be in the form of written statements, accompanied perhaps by photos, sketches, plans and diagrams or examples of weapons or other items used in the incident being investigated. It can also be provided by the spoken testimony of witnesses who claim to have observed the incident. As the court case does not take place immediately after the crime has been committed, it means that the collection of evidence can take some time, effort and preparation to compile. The old saying 'there are always two sides to every case' also applies to evidence of competent performance. So let us look at it first from the Assessor's viewpoint and, secondly, from the candidate's.

What will the Assessor be looking for?

Assessors need to understand all the issues that candidates face but they need also to be aware of their own specific responsibilities. The

Royal Society of Arts (RSA) is one of the main qualification-awarding bodies and they neatly summarise some of the Assessor's requirements for evidence as follows:

> **Many different types of evidence can be used. The crucial factor is that all the evidence must be valid. This means that evidence must relate directly and be appropriate for the competence that is being assessed and its associated performance criteria. A second factor is the sufficiency of the evidence. The Assessor must satisfy him/herself that there is sufficient evidence on which to make a judgement. If the statement of the range of situations indicates four different types of client groups, for example, in which the performance criteria must be demonstrated, it will not be sufficient for a candidate's evidence to refer only to one type of group.**
>
> **Wherever possible – since certification is based on occupational competence – assessment should take place in the real workplace. In some circumstances, it may be acceptable to use a realistic simulation of the workplace for assessment purposes.**
>
> **When making claims for achievement to an Assessor, candidates should produce supporting evidence, where appropriate. Whenever possible, this evidence should be drawn from naturally occurring work activities.**
>
> **The Accreditation of Prior Learning is similar to accreditation of current achievement in that it must be based on valid evidence. The only additional questions which need to be asked are those of:**
>
> - **authenticity (does the evidence belong to the candidate putting it forward?); and**
> - **currency (are the skills, knowledge and understanding which are evidenced by prior achievement still current?).**

The Management Charter Initiative (MCI) has been responsible for defining the performance standards for management functions. Collecting evidence in these situations is not so easily done by observation but, even if the collection methods may differ, the same principles of evidence apply. MCI also issue guidance notes. Their point about confidentiality is important:

> **Some organisations may be unwilling or unable to release certain documents due to legal requirements or the need to retain confidential data on employees or financial returns. If confidentiality presents a barrier to gathering the evidence needed, a letter of validation may be an appropriate second option. Or alternatively, it may be possible to delete certain information or recreate evidence in a different way, without of course breaking confidence. An**

Adviser or Assessor should be able to provide additional guidance about this matter.

An Assessor also has to be aware of some common errors that are quite easy to make when judging evidence. The National Council for Vocational Qualifications provided me with some examples. They point out that historical evidence is open to the following errors:

- it may be out of date;
- it may relate to performance against other incompatible standards;
- it may be evidence of group performance and thus data about an individual is difficult to identify.

Work performance data is subject to other errors:

- record-keeping and observations may be erratic due to work constraints;
- local standards may be incompatible with national standards;
- the assessment may be unduly influenced by prior knowledge of the candidate.

Performance data collected on specifically set tasks or assignments is subject to the following errors:

- too much may be inferred from the observations when assigning competence;
- one-off or short-term assignments may not give a true picture (someone who performs quickly may not be consistently accurate but someone who performs slowly may be very reliable);
- off-site assessments may not be representative because of unfamiliar surroundings.

The candidate's view

For candidates working towards a competence-based qualification, the situation is basically the same as collecting evidence for a court case. They will need direct evidence, produced by them and indirect evidence produced about them by others. Taken together, this should be adequate to prove their competence to an Assessor. One major difference exists in proving competence for a qualification. Where convenient and appropriate, the Assessor will want to observe a candidate performing the relevant tasks. Observed evidence in the workplace is often the best form of evidence for many qualifications and, whenever possible, an Assessor will prefer to judge it. Sometimes one Assessor will judge performance and then present a report to other Assessors. Although this becomes indirect evidence, it is still very strong evidence indeed.

Where do candidates find the evidence?

Evidence can come from a number of sources. As competence-based programmes are essentially workbased, the first question to ask is how much of the evidence is readily available in everyday workplace activities? By looking carefully at the precise wording of the units, elements and performance criteria, what can be shown of the work that the candidates already do that will prove that they do it competently? A careful look through the filing system for records of meetings, budget plans, analysis of training needs, compilation of manpower needs, etc may well be the kind of evidence needed. Alternatively, are there any examples of finished articles or photographs or videos of them?

A second important source of evidence will be from candidates' previous learning or experience. They may well have become competent at doing something in a previous job or through having learnt it and carried it out in the past. Is there any evidence that would show that they have already been 'tested' and found competent? If they can provide evidence to confirm prior learning, then that can also be presented to show competence. It is now possible to gain qualifications very largely based on the accreditation of prior learning.

A third source of evidence may come from special tasks designed to develop competence which might have been specially taken on in order to show that they are able to do something even if it is outside their immediate job description.

A fourth source of evidence will centre around the ability to answer questions to prove that candidates have the necessary knowledge and understanding to underpin the functions they are trying to prove competence in. For example, an Assessor may want to ask why they carried out a particular procedure; or what their actions would be if a different or similar situation arose. The ability to answer questions correctly and clearly will be an important consideration in persuading an Assessor.

To establish the best types of evidence for a particular situation, it is helpful to use a checklist. As an example, these are the questions a candidate might ask themselves which are suggested by City and

Guilds for the qualification in retail management for supervisors and managers:

1. Can I demonstrate my competence in any way that can be observed by a line manager or Assessor?
2. Have I any evidence of previous experience or learning?
3. Can I present a 'finished product' for assessment?
4. What documentation and records are completed and kept which would assist my claim of competence?
5. Could my line manager report on any aspect of my competence? (Any such report must be related directly to the unit of competence and it must be written and signed.)
6. Is the unit appropriate for the presentation of any visual evidence such as photography or video recording?
7. Could a case study help me to generate the evidence?
8. Could a project or assignment help in a similar way?
9. Will I need to answer any questions to ensure that all aspects of competence are covered?
10. Should I provide a written or tape-recorded personal account of my competence?

Collecting the evidence

In most cases it will probably need a combination of different kinds of evidence to prove competence. Some pieces of evidence can be used to prove more than one performance criterion, but one piece of evidence on its own will rarely be enough to prove a case.

While it will be important to consider what types and sources of evidence are relevant in the work situation, occasionally too, out-of-work evidence may be acceptable. For example, if a candidate chairs meetings of their local voluntary organisation but does not have a similar opportunity at work, they might use this as acceptable evidence. Candidates should not be afraid to examine or volunteer different types and sources of evidence. They should use imagination but always keep in mind the performance criteria that they are trying to prove.

Some pieces of evidence will be easier to gather than others, simply because they already exist in filing systems or because they use particular forms, specifications or documentation as part of daily work. Other pieces of evidence may be more difficult to locate. Some may need to be created. Some may require other people to be asked to provide indirect evidence about a candidate. It is for the latter pieces of evidence that the advice of a Coach, Mentor, Assessment Adviser or line manager may be necessary. The more organised a candidate is in planning the collection of evidence, the easier it will be to collect – a simple statement with a lot of practical experience to support it!

A useful technique is for candidates to keep an ongoing record of experiences in a work or diary log, or a day book. This is where they might record things not written down elsewhere, eg incidents or tasks which might contribute to proof. This might include thoughts after attending a training session or workshop or reflections on how they would react in a different situation, and so on. This log could be included in the portfolio of evidence, but is more likely to provide data that would be used to support and explain other evidence. It may also help as a reminder when the candidates have to answer questions at the assessment interview.

Presenting the evidence in a portfolio

The most common way of organising evidence so that it can easily be reviewed by an Assessor is to compile it into a portfolio. A portfolio for a competence-based qualification will contain a variety of inserts such as lists of achievements, curriculum vitae, examples of work, photographs, plans etc.

The portfolio of evidence is what the Assessor will receive in advance to evaluate before meeting the candidate for an interview or guided discussion to make the final judgement of competence. It follows that the most effective portfolio is likely to be one which speaks for itself and the least effective is that which is untidy, poorly organised and difficult to understand. If an Assessor finds a portfolio easy to follow, it will create a positive initial reaction.

Ensuring that a portfolio speaks for itself is the responsibility of the candidate. It is wise to assume that the Assessor may be an outsider and therefore is someone who does not share an intimate knowledge of the candidate's workplace or organisation. The terms and language used must be either self-explanatory or properly explained. For example, if a promotional deal is presented as a piece of evidence, will the Assessor know what a promotional deal is? And if so, does it follow that what the candidate has called a promotional deal is the same as that in another context? If minutes of meetings are included as evidence, the Assessor will need to know who else was involved and what was their relationship to the candidate. To explain this, it may be necessary to provide not only an organisational plan, but also a note to show that the meeting occurred within the work situation and how it relates to the performance criterion being proved.

Documents included in a portfolio must also be able to show *why* they have been included. It will not be sufficient just to include everything that touches on a performance criterion. Documents have got to be shown to be relevant. It will help for a candidate to ask constantly 'Will this evidence speak clearly for itself to someone who does not understand the situation as well as I do?' If the answer to that question is 'maybe', then the candidate will have to help it speak for itself by adding a personal statement or explanatory note.

To help evidence speak for itself, always go back to the precise wording of the performance criteria and the statements of evidence requirements which accompany them. Does the performance criterion ask for evidence of how the candidate actually did something, or simply contributed to it, or aided others, or prepared something, or kept people informed and so on? Every verb, adverb and adjective in the performance criteria wording is important. Words like 'appropriately informed' can change the complexion of what is needed as evidence. The judgement may rest on the Assessor's interpretation of 'appropriately', as much as on 'informed'.

It is the candidate's choice as to what goes into a portfolio of evidence. An Adviser, Coach, Mentor or workplace Assessor may offer guidance, support or advice, but ultimately candidates are responsible for their own work. Assessors, of course, have to pay particular attention to checking the authenticity of evidence.

There are no set requirements for the design of portfolios, but a flexible format is probably best. Usually the portfolio takes the form of one or more ring-binders or lever-arch files, subdivided by unit. Some Assessors have suggested that it is useful to have two files: one containing the personal statements, explanatory notes, organisational charts and the other containing the evidence in terms of memos, reports, brochures etc. Assessors may well look at the first file in some detail, dipping into the second as they see fit.

Each entry in a portfolio should have its own unique identifying number. The portfolio should then be fronted by a matrix (see Figure 3.1) which shows clearly which piece of evidence relates to which performance criterion, element and unit. Some pieces of evidence may be relevant to more than one performance criterion, hence the need for clear identifiers on each sheet of paper and the matrix.

FIG 3.1 CROSS REFERENCING FORM

Performance element 5.2

Reference number	Description	a	b	c	d	e	f	g	h	i	j
d1		✓		✓		✓					
d2		✓	✓	✓	✓	✓	✓	✓	✓	✓	✓

(Performance criteria: a–j)

To make the portfolio even more user friendly, it is useful to include a list of contents, registration form (if any), development plans, and other relevant background information.

How to get started

This is a reasonable question. But first a word of caution. Before you begin, it would be wise to read the chapters on the role of the Coach, Mentor and Assessor. Depending on the situation, discussion with one or more of them before a candidate starts to collect evidence will be important. One of the first questions they ask may well be – 'Is the qualification you are aiming for appropriate?' Remember, candidates have to present evidence of what they can do. If their current experience and present job is unlikely to cover all the performance standards, then an additional separate development plan will be needed. Alternatively they might aim for a different qualification which more closely matches their immediate potential.

Let us assume for our purposes that the candidate has chosen an appropriate level of qualification to aim for and that a certain number of units have been selected and the individual elements identified. Experience shows that only a carefully planned programme will produce an organised presentation of evidence. Inevitably, therefore, a quite detailed planning process has to be devised. As the candidates may wish to include the planning process as part of their evidence portfolio, it should also be paper-based. Everyone will have their own planning preferences but the basic approach can be explained and summarised on one form as illustrated on Figure 3.2.

To complete the form, the candidates will need to ensure that they understand thoroughly the performance criteria for each element. Using one page of the planner per element and physically writing in each performance criterion will help reinforce their knowledge. The next stage is to decide what sources of evidence are most appropriate to prove competence for each performance criterion in the element. The following types of evidence will be available; the candidates need to choose the combination that best suits their case. If they need to complete a special assignment to generate evidence or if they need more practice or training before they can generate evidence, this can be indicated also. The types of evidence are:

1. Demonstration or observed performance
2. Finished or end product
3. Work documents or records
4. Visuals, eg video, photos, etc
5. Records of recent projects, assignments or from work diary
6. Reports from line managers
7. Report from coach
8. Report from others
9. Report from the candidate (this will always be required, at the very least to explain the other evidence to the Assessor)
10. Examples from home, social activities or voluntary work
11. Responding to questions or guided discussion led by the Assessor
12.* A special assignment needed because the candidate has not done this before

FIG 3.2 EVIDENCE PLANNER

PERFORMANCE ELEMENT 9.1 Lead meetings and group discussions to solve problems and make decisions

PERFORMANCE CRITERIA			TYPES OF EVIDENCE										
	1	2	3	4	5	6	7	8	9	10	11	12	13
Suitable No. of appropriate people invited	18/3				17/3						16/3		
Purpose of meeting established from outset	18/3		16/3	15/3				17/3					
Info. presented clearly & at appropriate time	1/3					3/3	1/3						
Leadership style helps others contribute fully								10/3			10/3		
Unhelpful digressions effectively discouraged	11/3							10/3			8/3		
Any decisions taken fall with group authority			21/3			18/3							
Decisions recorded accurately		15/3	15/3			18/3							
Decisions passed on to relevant people			1/3		28/2		28/2		3/3				

KEY:

1 Demonstration or observed performance
2 Finished or end product
3 Work documents or records
4 Visuals, e.g. video, photos, etc.
5 Records of recent projects, assignments or from work diary
6 Report from line-managers
7 Report from coach
8 Report from others
9 Report from yourself (this will always be required at a minimum to explain the other evidence to the Assessor)
10 Examples from home, social activities or voluntary work
11 Responding to questions or guided discussion led by Assessor
12 I will need a special assignment because I haven't done this before
13 I need more practice or training before I can generate evidence

INSTRUCTIONS

First, fill in the name of the element at the top of the form. Enter the performance criteria in the left hand column. Then, with the aid of the key, decide which types of evidence will be available. For each performance criterion mark a date by which the collection will be completed under the relevant types of evidence. Remember also to check the appropriate Range Statements.

13.* More practice or training needed before candidate can generate evidence

*Both the last two types of evidence will need a separate development plan.

Candidates should not just tick the appropriate boxes but should also enter the date by which they will complete the collection of the evidence. They can then tick the box when the evidence has been agreed with their Adviser as suitable for submitting in the evidence portfolio.

I recommend a separate page to plan for each element. As the overall intention may be to go for two or three units at a time, it can be seen that candidates will use between perhaps 15 and 20 pages to prepare a complete plan. A ring-binder and an overall summary chart will therefore also be useful. I prefer to lay out my summary chart as visually as possible (Figure 3.3). Other approaches may well suit individual styles and preferences better.

The process may sound easy and in a sense it is. But it disguises the volume of work involved and the sustained commitment candidates are going to need. The process I have outlined and illustrated allows candidates to establish how competent they are currently and precisely what they would have to do to develop their competence to become qualified when judged against the national standards. This route is not for the faint hearted. But whenever was it easy to gain qualifications that really mattered?

FIG 3.3 EVIDENCE PORTFOLIO CALENDAR

Week ending:	15/3	22/3	29/3	5/4	12/4	19/4	26/4	3/5	10/5	17/5	24/5	31/5	7/6	14/6	21/6	28/6	5/7	12/7
UNIT 1																		
Element 1																		
Element 2																		
Element 3																		
UNIT 2																		
Element 1																		
Element 2																		
Element 3																		
UNIT 3																		
Element 1																		
Element 2																		
Element 3																		

INSTRUCTIONS

Transfer the information from your Evidence Planner to show the start and completion date for each element. It is recommended that you tackle only one or two units at a time. This calendar will be the basis for regular review sessions.

CHAPTER 4
What Do I Have to Do if I am a Coach?

The *Concise Oxford Dictionary* defines coaching as 'to tutor, to train, to give hints, to prime with facts'. Until very recently I suspect that 80–90 per cent of people at work would not have recognised or used the word 'coaching' in any of these senses to apply to their daily working lives. The minority, most probably managers who have received some formal training, perhaps would remember that coaching was defined and taught as one of the various styles or activities that were part of every manager's job. Some of them would have put this into practice, particularly in those few organisations that place great emphasis on coaching.

But coaching does take place almost every day in every work situation. People do ask their colleagues and managers to show, explain or advise them how to do certain aspects of their job or how to do things better. This type of coaching is mostly haphazard and unstructured and the resulting improvements in performance often equally so.

In the current climate, the recognition of the need for, and improvement in, coaching practice will, I believe, increase substantially. This will be driven in part by the economic imperative to increase the level and effectiveness of training. Organisations will recognise that one of the most cost effective ways to achieve this is to use the talent and expertise of the existing workforce. Relying on external help to do the complete job will inevitably be too general and too expensive. Technology and flexible learning packages can provide an inexpensive way of helping to meet the increased demand. But experience has shown that these techniques, without skilled coaching support from internal management, rarely fulfil their potential.

Another pressure will come from learners themselves. The whole ethos of how you become educated, trained and developed is changing. Passive learning and parrot-like repetition of facts and theories in an examination room will become a thing of the past. Learners' expectations, preferences and needs will exert increasing pressure on organisations to use their internal expertise in ways and at times convenient to both coach and learner. Giving managers and specialists explicit coaching responsibilities will become widespread. By the year 1995, my guess is that more than 50 per cent of people at work will recognise and benefit from systematic coaching.

Who should coach?

Anyone in an organisation with a special expertise or with supervisory or management responsibility could be required to act as a Coach. Those who believe strongly that it should be the manager or supervisor alone who should undertake the role should listen to David Kenney, the Management Development Manager for 2,000 Boots the Chemist stores, who says:

> 'We emphasise that it is fundamentally the manager's responsibility but, historically, only some of our managers accept this and even fewer do it. But attitudes are changing and it is part of my mission to ensure that 100 per cent of our managers behave as good coaches.'

David is at the leading edge and is well aware of the task he has set himself. For many others the experience is that busy managers, even if they have the inclination, rarely feel they have the time to spend with an underperforming member of the team. Day-to-day job pressures also mean that even new team members sometimes only get minimal help.

This sad reality will only change if people are given specific responsibility within their job definition to do coaching. This responsibility need not be only for their own workgroup. Someone with special expertise and coaching skills could be used to improve performance in several parts of the organisation. Of course, training specialists should be an obvious coaching resource. If they are acceptable and have the time, they should be used. Experience suggests, however, that trainers are often too thin on the ground or more usefully used in developing, organising and evaluating the whole range of training programmes, including coaching. External consultants are another resource. But they are best used to act as Coaches and facilitators, not to run traditional training courses.

The key roles

The best way to explain coaching is first to describe the roles and processes. Then use examples from work and other activities like music, dancing and sport, where the role of the coach is well established and familiar. The skills required will then become apparent.

My experience suggests that there are four main coaching roles that need to be understood:

- 'hands-on' when working with inexperienced learners;
- 'hands-off' when developing higher performance with experienced learners;
- 'supporter' when helping learners use a flexible learning package technique; and
- 'qualifier' when helping a learner develop a specific requirement for a competence-based or professional qualification.

The first two roles, 'hands-on' and 'hands-off' are really two ends of the same coaching continuum. In between there are variations on the roles which should be adopted solely in relation to the experience and needs of the learner in the same way that a driving instructor judges when to take his hands and feet off the controls or jam them on.

For a newcomer to a job, or for someone inexperienced who requires to tackle a problem instantly, the 'hands-on' Coach might well say 'I am going to tell you exactly what to do. I will show you how to do it. Do exactly what I do. Is that clear? Now start and now stop. That was good (or bad or indifferent). Now do it again. Right, now you know how to do it, so carry on.'

This type of coaching may be completely appropriate in some situations. The tone and style, of course, need to be sympathetic and motivational. But the clarity of expression and simplicity of explanation is essential. For those who have been trained as instructors, the similarity of this approach to what is often termed basic 'one-to-one' instruction will be obvious.

For someone who is highly experienced and qualified or who is already a very good performer but wants to become an even better one, the 'hands-off' coaching role may be appropriate. This Coach may well say 'Can you tell me what your performance goals are? Are they realistic, stretching, achievable, measurable? How do you plan to achieve them? What options do you have? What help will you need? Can you show me? How does it feel? Can you imagine what success might be like? Can you describe it?'

This Coach is relying almost entirely on questioning to enable learners to develop their own improvement plan and to own the responsibility for achieving it, and at the same time developing the mental attitude necessary for success. The origins of this approach can be traced back to ancient Greece where Socrates used it. Questioning, Socrates advocated, was the appropriate technique to help the student discover for themselves what they needed to know. In more recent times, writers, like Tim Gallwey in his book *The Inner Game of Tennis*, have applied new psychological and philosophical insights and adapted questioning and self-development techniques into a practical process of self-awareness and mental conditioning for sportsmen and for people at work. It is a book all coaches could usefully read and I discuss it again in the chapter on giving feedback which builds confidence and success.

Coaching in action

Let us now look at some examples of people who have been involved in coaching in real-life situations.

Myra Ashworth is the Vocational Training Manager for the national DIY retail chain B & Q. Most of the supervisors in each of around 300 stores have to be trained to coach new starters to reach the performance standards laid down in the City and Guilds qualification levels 1 and 2 for store-operative skills. Myra explains:

> 'The approach we use at B & Q certainly begins very close to the "hands-on" coaching role. We are developing basic competencies and it is relatively easy to recognise when people have acquired the basic skills. So the approach is appropriate. When we move on to develop the Supervisors' or Managers' competence, we are not dealing with beginners, so we have to adjust our approach. In this case, the Coach is more likely to be helping a candidate "top up" in order to reach the performance objectives and a range of people might be involved – Assessors, District Managers, Store Managers, Assistant Managers or more experienced Supervisors.'

Mark Poulter of B & Q was coached to help him gain the NVQ level 1 and 2 qualifications. Mark explained the way it worked:

> 'First of all we worked out what I could and couldn't already do. Then we made a checklist of those elements that I either had no experience in or needed to brush up on. Each week we'd try and tick something off the list by setting aside an hour or two for my manager to explain and show me how it was done and for me to practise and get used to it.
>
> 'What I like about my situation is that I feel my manager has my best interests at heart. If he thinks I'm not doing something right he will tell me. I can always ask him for help if I get stuck on something.'

Cameron Burness, a production plant manager with ICI Pharmaceuticals, fully believes that coaching is an integral part of management. He is always on the lookout for coaching opportunities:

> 'I don't actually need to be a technical expert in everything that my 100 or so staff might be doing. Being able to listen and ask the right questions, quickly to understand a problem and give positive feedback is what I see as my coaching responsibility. I find the experience–reflection–conclusion–action loop to be a sound method to follow which, in fact, applies to almost all coaching situations that I find myself in.
>
> 'Everything I do is essentially performance-aimed. I use coaching as a means of getting my staff to a level where I can delegate work to them which I would otherwise have to do myself. I see the time I spend coaching very much as an investment the dividend from which is the far greater time I save myself through delegation.'

David Thompson, a partner in accountants KPMG Peat Marwick, sees coaching as:

> 'part of the fundamental ethos of our firm. Student accountants have to gain experience on real-life client assignments. This means they have to be coached by their senior who, in turn, will have been coached by a manager or partner. Client satisfaction and working within a budget forces us to coach effectively. In practice, people try to ensure their teams have the best qualified staff which reduces the coaching load on managers. But cutting corners on coaching overall can be an expensive mistake.'
>
> David Clifford, another partner of the firm, adds:

'Everyone from the second-year student upwards takes on a coaching role at times. Even senior partners, though they may not recognise it as such, are coached by each other. For example, if I'm working on a report and have some ideas that I'm not completely sure about, I might test them out on a fellow partner who will then give me advice and feedback. Of course, coaching is more obvious when you're explaining something to a junior member of staff but the type of coaching I've just described goes on every day and without it we wouldn't be one of the top accountancy firms in the country.'

Nursing is a profession where learning is a continuing and fundamental part of the job. Sally Bassett, a senior sister at the Westminster Hospital in London, explains:

'A large part of my daily work could be called coaching although we use the terms teaching and role modelling. But even a newly qualified staff nurse has to be able to coach student nurses and clearly a 'hands-on' role is required initially when the penalty for a mistake can be unnecessary pain for a patient. In my own case, I have to keep up to date with new developments and, while I would expect some hands-on coaching during a demonstration, I respond much better to a hands-off approach as I put things into practice.'

Garnet Marshall, director of instructor training at the British School of Motoring said:

'Training at BSM is going through a total change of ethos. We think that coaching is a better way of learning than the old-fashioned autocratic way of standing up in front of people. We're aiming for a situation where everyone is coached in a way that encourages them to find things out for themselves. I don't want to be in the business of force-feeding people knowledge. In order to create the right environment for people to learn, the trainer must become a facilitator.'

Terry, a BSM driving instructor in Brighton, clearly recognised the hands-on to hands-off coaching spectrum in his job. He must take a complete beginner who may never have sat behind a wheel before through a test to become a competent, road safe driver.

'The first few lessons are really just instruction rather than coaching in its fullest sense. But about halfway through the series of

> lessons, the learner has been taught or shown everything they need to know. From then on it's a matter of practising and perfecting. This is where I suppose it becomes more hands-off – and feet off. Believe me, I wouldn't be alive now if I didn't have dual controls! At this stage, I just try and let them drive without interfering. If they make a mistake, I'll tell them and then get them to try and work out what it was and why it happened. If it's a major mistake then we'll pull over and analyse what went wrong'.

Joan Sutherland, the Australian opera singer, actually married her coach! She met Richard Bonynge in 1951 when she entered the Royal College of Music. He was doing advanced study at the time. He spotted her great talent and began to coach her. At first this was in the form of friendly advice but gradually it became more and more formal. One famous coaching technique he used to develop and extend her voice was to sit at the piano in a position where she could not see the keys. By getting her to copy the notes he played, he took her beyond her imagined limit of high C! They married on 16 October 1954.

Sir John Whitmore, a former European motor racing champion, is one who has developed *The Inner Game of Tennis*' ideas into practical coaching success from supervisors to main board directors. His focus is developing a deep sense of self-awareness and self-coaching. He quotes Tim Gallwey, saying: 'The opponent in your head is often more daunting than your opponent on the other side of the net.'

David Hemery, the former Olympic 400m hurdles champion, has spent many years researching, developing and practising coaching in sport and business. He has a fund of interesting stories. He compares his own gold medal track performance at the Mexico Olympics in 1968 with that of Lyn Davies in the long jump at the same games. Both were superbly fit and had received extensive coaching.

Davies had won the gold medal at the previous Olympics in Tokyo. He knew his main competitors well and their potential performance. He was also intensely competitive and felt he could beat them. He was proud of his will to win the gold again. That was his focus. Almost as soon as the competition began Bob Beamon, a little-known American athlete, produced a jump that not only beat the world record but exceeded everyone's expectations of what was possible. Davies knew he couldn't beat it. His confidence evaporated. He finished last, producing a below average performance. He had set himself no other goal than to win.

Hemery and his coach on the other hand had planned his approach meticulously for months. The schedule included milestones for qualifying times, team selection, positioning in the heats and the semi-finals. Hemery wanted to win the gold. He calculated that to do so he had to run faster than anyone had run before. That became his goal in the final. That is how he ran the race. He exceeded his performance goal, won the race - and also the gold medal which had been his ultimate goal.

The importance he and his coach placed on planning a schedule and clear goal-setting was confirmed. This is also vital in the work situation. Involving your boss in the process is important too. Only if management agree with the time required and with the goals to be achieved will they allow the space for the coach and learner to work.

Another successful sports Coach is David Whitaker who has translated his success with the British Hockey team in the Seoul Olympics into business coaching. His experience is with team coaching. He explains:

> 'Teams require individual and small group coaching as well as whole team coaching sessions. The Coach knows he is being successful when the players take over the coaching sessions themselves. This allows the Coach to "helicopter" above the team and take an overall view. Interventions become more selective and are expressed in a way that doesn't disturb the ownership of responsibility among the players for their own performance. The really effective Coach works himself out of the job. My team talk before the gold medal final in Seoul was simply "I know that you know what you are going to do - good luck". They did and they won.'

Case Study

Carolyn Robertson is a former regional sales manager from the pharmaceutical industry and, latterly, a management consultant. She describes herself as 'an enthusiast about work but passionate about eventing'. This is a report of her experience:

Carolyn not only enjoyed her chosen sport, one-day eventing, a great deal, but she soon realised that she had the potential to try and compete at the highest level. Recognising the need for specialist coaching, she turned to an experienced horse-riding trainer for help. Steady progress was made over a five-year period and she was achieving modest success in competitions. But gradually her coaching yielded fewer and fewer improvements. In an attempt to improve, a change of horse was recommended, but still no results. She became frustrated and lacking in self-confidence. Her relationship with her Coach became strained and she began to give up her ambition of being successful at eventing. Finally, she decided to change her Coach in a last attempt to rediscover her form.

The new Coach introduced very different learning methods and, after only a few weeks, significant progress was being made. The new approach was very much a hands-off style of coaching. It began with a four-day assessment of horse and rider, both together and individually. An action plan, divided into stages, was agreed. Each stage was completed when the agreed level of competence was reached. Carolyn was asked to keep a diary of all activities, thoughts and self-analyses which was then brought to the session for discussion. The emphasis here was on self-reflection which, apart from being a valuable exercise in itself, also saved time. 'I now realise that, when lack of progress becomes evident, time must be taken to analyse and explain the cause. Through discussion, a plan of action should be agreed.'

These formal coaching sessions would be structured around a series of key questions: 'What are you trying to achieve? Is that what you are achieving? But what about . . . ? What are you going to do to get where you want to be? Let me tell you what I feel about it.' Forcing her focus on to what her objectives should be in this way encouraged her to take responsibility for everything that happened.

However, like most real-life coaching situations, there were times when such a single coaching style was not always appropriate. For example, a much more hands-on role was adopted when tackling new or particularly difficult areas. When this was the case (perhaps in relation to a particular manoeuvre), verbal explanation was given by the Coach as to what was needed and how it was to be done. Carolyn would first try the movement on her own; the coach would then demonstrate what was happening and what should be happening. Carolyn would copy the Coach and then repeat it on her own and they would return to the problem area at the end of the session to check the earlier learning had been retained.

During all coaching sessions, though, continuous evaluation and assessment was taking place with time-frames and short-term goals constantly being set and reset in the light of progress. It was vital that success and achievement was recognised. Carolyn was also inspired to spend time researching the theory of successful riding which she saw as part of her own self-coaching development.

Apart from finding this type of coaching enjoyable and challenging, Carolyn found her confidence had increased. She had a deeper understanding of processes and the causes of mistakes. Most importantly, she became able to take corrective action of her own accord. This was in stark contrast to her previous experience of coaching when she felt she was not taken seriously or given 100 per cent attention by her Coach. On reflection, she feels this might have been because she was seen as a threat by him as she became better than he was. 'The pupil must feel that the Coach has confidence in his or her abilities.' Her new Coach, it seems, had found the right balance: 'Coaches must take into account the pupil's experience but, at the same time, not make assumptions, especially if the pupil's circumstances change.'

As well as having the right technique, Carolyn also believes that the Coach's attitude is vital to success: 'The pupil must feel able to ask the most basic of questions which means no Coach should put themselves out of reach physically or intellectually. Honesty, trust, empathy and respect are key words in any coaching partnership.'

After five years, Carolyn clearly needed to be taking an important step forward in her coaching and, while she recognised that almost any change at that time would have helped, the new methods, more appropriate to her experience, ability and preferred learning style, have helped her enormously.

Performance tasks and skills

The case study and practical examples confirm the hands-on–hands-off roles as two ends of the same coaching continuum. They also illustrate the need for Coaches to be truly flexible in positioning themselves on this continuum to match their learners' needs, even within a single coaching session. To achieve this 'seamless performance' a Coach needs to be aware of the full range of the coaching continuum. It is possible to establish a basic process which applies to all situations. Like many other management processes, it follows a simple problem-solving model.

FIG 4.1 COACHING MODEL

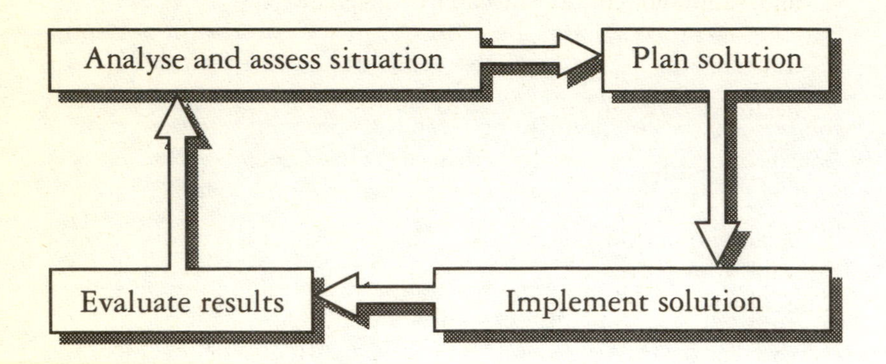

It is also possible to describe the process in performance terms. That is, specific outcomes that a coach would have to produce. Describing the process in this way obviously links in to the way that competent performance can be assessed and, eventually, qualifications gained. The competent Coach has to perform the following tasks:

Analyse

- assess current standards of performance
- identify learning needs to meet performance goals and required standards

Plan

- identify and organise suitable learning resource(s) and opportunities
- agree learning plans, coaching role and assessment methods
- provide opportunities for individuals and groups to manage their own learning

Implement

- explain, demonstrate and supervise practice of concepts and techniques
- ensure opportunities for feedback and discussion

- adjust coaching role and programme to suit learners' needs and progress
- demonstrate awareness of Health and Safety, Equal Opportunities and Employment Law and Special Needs issues

Evaluate

- evaluate achievement of goals and standards
- provide feedback, encouragement and support to individuals to apply learning

To be able to perform these tasks, the competent Coach will need the relevant knowledge and a set of skills. These can be classed as core skills which are also common to mentoring and assessing; technique skills which relate to each learner being coached; and personal skills which relate to the style and tone of the Coach's behaviour. These skills too can be described in performance terms and specific performance criteria can be established. However, these skills are more likely to be seen as underlying and underpinning skills rather than performance that will be formally assessed for a coaching qualification.

Core skills

- listen attentively
- observe and recognise competent performance
- demonstrate effective questioning technique
- respond, summarise and clarify situations

Technique skills

- recognise different learning styles
- adapt to preferred learning styles
- adopt appropriate coaching roles
- gain acceptance and commitment to performance goals from learner

Personal skills

- display sensitivity to and empathy for learners' thoughts and ideas and need for appropriate feedback
- establish rapport and good communication channels with learner
- encourage learner to take responsibility for own development
- support and build confidence in learner

Specialist roles

The basic coaching process and the necessary knowledge and skills also apply to the other two main coaching roles we have identified, 'the supporter' and 'the qualifier'. These two roles are each significantly different in the sense that they require additional tasks to be performed as well as needing additional knowledge and skills. Both roles will become increasingly important in the context of developing competence among the workforce.

The supporter

We have defined the supporter role as coaching when helping learners to use a flexible learning package. This method of learning will become more widespread. The packages are a very inexpensive way of providing learners with a body of learning resource when compared to the cost of full-time tutors and classroom-based activities. The learner can choose both the way that they would like to use the learning resources in line with their own learning styles and also the time and pace to suit the pressures of their environment.

But this method of learning also has some drawbacks to balance the advantages of the cost, convenience and flexibility to suit personal preferences. Although the packages come in various formats, they often involve some new form of technology. This may be a video cassette, a computer disk or a modern interactive compact disc. For some people, technology is still a worry. Knowing how to use it or what to do if it appears not to work can be quite stressful. Access to a human being who can 'sort it out' is seen as a great advantage.

This is the simplest form of support needed, but much more is required. Years of experience from organisations who have used learning packages – from correspondence courses, through programmed learning, to interactive video workstations – strongly suggests that the single most common reason for them not realising their potential is lack of human support from internal management. This has been largely because of an attitude problem among managers. The virtues of packaged learning have often been seen as a way of letting learners get on with it without bothering busy managers. Sometimes packages have been bought as a conscious alternative to employing expensive trainers. This has been a false way to tackle the economics of effective training and development.

Flexible packages do not remove the need for human support. They change the balance and nature of support required. They allow the learners in their own time to acquire much of the knowledge, techniques and skills previously delivered by tutors in the classroom. This then makes more time available for the individual and group interaction, discussion and coaching that was always needed but never provided sufficiently to develop genuine competence. This type of coaching support is essential. It need not be provided by a trainer or a specialist in the subject matter. A Coach who is readily available, and knows how to help learners apply what they are learning by skilful questioning and feedback, will do the job well. A skilled Coach can also organise, or help the learner organise workshops or action learning groups where other learners can work together to relate their individual learning programmes to each other's experiences.

The combination of coaching and flexible learning packages will suit some situations extremely well. The Coaches will need to follow the basic coaching process. In addition, they will need to perform the following tasks:

- explain how flexible packages can be used to good effect;
- demonstrate the use of any technology involved;
- agree and organise the appropriate level of support for the learner;
- organise facilitation of workshops and action learning groups as appropriate.

To be able to perform these tasks, the supporter Coach will need a good working knowledge of flexible learning packages and their associated technology. But the only additional skill required, again expressed in performance terms, will be to lead and facilitate workshops and action learning groups.

Someone who has extensive experience of gaining maximum benefit from flexible learning packages is Les Ratcliffe, the senior training officer from Jaguar Cars. The Jaguar Open Learning Centres were established in 1983. More than 4,500 learners have taken advantage of a range of more than 100 courses. Even during the recent recession Jaguar retained their commitment to open learning. Les Ratcliffe explains:

> 'The real flexibility of our Learning Centres is the main reason for continuing support from the company during recent difficult times. Coaching, however, has enabled this flexible learning undertaken by individual employees to be transferred to the

workplace. It is normally the supervisor, acting as a Coach and guide, who has helped put the learning experience into practice. By far the most successful programmes have been those supported by effective coaching.'

The qualifier

The fourth main coaching role is that of 'the qualifier'. This will apply usually in situations where a candidate for a competence-based or professional qualification identifies a specific performance task in which they need to develop competence as part of a larger qualification programme. A typical situation might be for a candidate to develop competence in preparing a marketing plan, using a spreadsheet, chairing a meeting or inputting and retrieving information from a database. The request will probably have arisen from a candidate's discussions with either their Mentor or Assessment Adviser. The need will have been identified but neither the Mentor nor Adviser is in a position to provide the specific development required.

To fulfil this role, the Coach will, of course, employ the normal coaching process. But to develop an appropriate coaching plan, the Coach will require a detailed knowledge of the relevant qualification process and the standards and performance criteria for the task to be performed. As all competence-based qualification programmes require the candidate to submit a portfolio of evidence to demonstrate competence, the Coach will need to be familiar with the requirements of the particular awarding body involved. Unfortunately, although all awarding bodies apply similar criteria for similar performance tasks, not all awarding bodies at the moment have identical assessment and evidence requirements for every award. Over time, there will be a convergence of practice between bodies. In the meantime, the Coach must be aware of what is required. The Assessment Adviser is the most likely source of this information.

The need for the Coach to liaise closely with a candidate's Mentor, Adviser and manager is more important in this role. It is, of course, desirable in any coaching situation where the Coach is someone other than a learner's manager. Gaining a qualification will be neither a particularly easy nor a rapid process for the candidate. The 'qualifier' Coach will need to see their role as being part of the team helping the candidate. As in all team situations good communication between members is an important ingredient for success.

So too is focus. In this role, the Coach may be focussing on a relatively small part of the candidate's needs. The timescale may be shorter but any programme will need to be properly coordinated with other activities.

Paula Wills is the Training Manager for the newly privatised North West Water Authority. She has specific responsibility for the graduate intake, most of whom are keen to obtain further qualifications. North West Water use a combination of Mentors and Coaches to help graduates develop the necessary range of skills. Paula explains:

> 'Each graduate will have a Mentor who is likely to be a senior manager whom we have selected for their skill as a Mentor. We do not expect them all to have the experience of every part of the organisation. But it is their job to ensure that the line manager to whom the graduate is assigned is capable of providing the coaching; either themselves or by appointing a specialist from within the department. This system works well but does require a widespread appreciation of the coaching role.'

The additional tasks that the 'qualifier' Coach will need to perform are to:

- explain clearly the standards and performance criteria required for the specific qualification desired
- enable the candidate to collect and present appropriate evidence for assessment
- liaise effectively with other people supporting the candidate's qualification programme

The Coach will require detailed knowledge of the professional or competence-based qualification programme. The evidence requirements will be particularly important. The one additional skill required for this role compared to the other roles is to be able to build good working relationships with team members in various parts of the organisation.

Summary, checklist and references

Taking all four coaching roles together, we have developed 17 general and specialist performance tasks and 14 matching sets of skills required to develop a competent Coach. Elsewhere in the book, we look in more detail at the performance criteria against which evidence must be produced to demonstrate competent coaching. But the following checklist may provide a useful summary of the most important points.

Checklist

1. Start every session with an agreed goal for that session that relates to other previously agreed goals.
2. Plan and prepare each session in advance to ensure that adequate time and resources are available.
3. If you have to demonstrate concepts or techniques, keep it short and simple.
4. While a 'hands-on' role is appropriate for inexperienced learners, move as quickly as possible to the 'hands-off' role as it encourages greater ownership of the development process by the learner.
5. If you are in a 'qualifier' or 'supporter' role, do your homework thoroughly in advance.
6. Remember that, while questioning may be your most important skill, observing and listening are also vital skills.
7. Feedback should be positive and encouraging and criticism always presented constructively.
8. Allow plenty of opportunities for discussion and review of performance goals in the light of progress achieved.
9. Respect and liaise constantly with other people involved in helping the learner develop.
10. Aim to become qualified yourself and recognise that coaching is a constant learning process for yourself.

Useful reference sources

The Inner Game of Tennis by Tim Gallwey
Pursuit of Sporting Excellence by David Hemery
The Winning Mind by John Whitmore

(Full details of these and other titles relevant to each chapter can be found in appendix 1 on p. 154.)

CHAPTER 5
What Do I Have to Do if I am a Mentor?

Mentor was the name of a character from Greek mythology who was a wise and trusted adviser or counsellor. The word has, until recently, kept that meaning. It is a word that is often used by politicians, sports people, actors and other performers to describe the person who they chose as a role model or someone who had a significant early influence on their professional careers.

In my own case I can identify an uncle, a friend who was successful in business, and a non-executive chairman who have all played a mentoring role for me. They played this role at different times in differing degrees and for different lengths of time. Two of them I selected myself rather unconsciously, the other one was politely imposed on me. All three helped me considerably but at no time did we use the term Mentor to each other; it just happened. My experience, I suspect, mirrors many others and left to itself, mentoring would have gone on in this way as it has for hundreds of years.

But times have changed. Mentoring has become a 'business buzzword'. Imported from America in the late 1980s it has become a 'flavour of the month'. Still worse, it has also become a 'vocational verb'. To Mentor is now a formal activity inextricably linked with the movement towards competence-based vocational qualifications. We need to understand these developments to know what mentoring entails.

Clarity or confusion?

David Clutterbuck is one of Britain's most prolific writers on management issues. In his book *Everyone Needs a Mentor*, published by the Institute of Personnel Management, he explains:

> Mentoring to some is a new and highly effective means of identifying and developing high-flyers; to others it is a means of speeding and facilitating the induction of young people in general. It can also be seen as an effective door into middle and senior management for women subject to unfair discrimination. Finally to some it is viewed as a dangerous process that can amplify favouritism and exclusive networks within the corporation. Mentoring, which inspires these widely differing interpretations, was an unknown term until the late 1970s. It is now the subject of intense academic study and widespread experimentation, particularly in the United States.
>
> In spite of the variety of definitions of mentoring (and the variety of names it is given, from coaching or counselling to sponsorship) all the experts and communicators appear to agree that it has its origins in the concept of apprenticeship, when an older, more experienced individual passed down his knowledge of how the task was done and how to operate in the commercial world.

The Council of National Academic Awards (CNAA) and the government Training Agency published an excellent report of research into the practical implications of assessing competence. The report discussed mentoring in these terms:

> There are many views and definitions of the role of Mentor, but all include verbs like support, guide, facilitate, etc. Important aspects are to do with listening, questioning and enabling, as distinct from telling, directing and restricting. Mentors are crucial to good management development since they can exert great influence in developing attitudes and encouraging good managerial practice. These are the messages from our research in the field, but it is also clear that being a Mentor is not an easy task and, in certain programmes, candidates were critical of the inexperience and unavailability of Mentors.
>
> High quality mentoring is concerned with competence, experience and clear role-definition, but it also crucially depends upon the right balance of personal qualities. One institution we surveyed encapsulates most of the evidence from the project when stating that good Mentors are:
>
> 1. good motivators, perceptive, able to support the objectives of the programme and fulfil their responsibilities to the candidate;
> 2. high performers, secure in their own position within the organisation and unlikely to feel threatened by, or resentful of, the candidate's opportunities;
> 3. able to show that a responsibility for mentoring is part of their own job description;

4. **able to establish a good and professional relationship, be sympathetic, accessible and knowledgeable about the candidate's area of interest;**
5. **sufficiently senior to be in touch with the corporate structure, sharing the company's values and able to give the candidate access to resources and information;**
6. **good teachers, able to advise and instruct without interfering, allowing candidates to explore and pursue ideas even though they may not be optimum pathways;**
7. **good negotiators, willing and able to plan alongside their own management teams and academics.**

In another exercise the government Training Agency and a specialist company Flexitrain Ltd consulted with numerous Mentors in different organisations to produce a training package. One interesting feature of this research is that the Mentors reported what they were *not*: 'We are not specialised subject tutors, social workers, specific appointments, reporting officers, all-powerful/omnipotent, paid extra, counsellors or welfare officers.'

Faced with this bewildering set of descriptions and definitions, it is tempting for people wanting to establish mentoring to conclude that mentoring in the work context can mean anything you like to describe it as. In a sense this should not surprise us. What we are involved in is a revolution in education and training with new practices and processes being articulated and applied. It will take time for clear definitions and use of terminology to become established. In another sense, I believe the confusion is unhelpful and, in part, this book is an attempt to provide some of the definitions that are needed.

Mentoring defined

Coaching and mentoring are similar activities and in the work context you can be called upon to fulfil both roles. But they are also distinct activities and you and the person you are coaching or mentoring need to understand the distinction. Once the distinction of roles is clear, it frankly does not matter too much what you call them.

The origin of both words is a good starting point. Coaching is derived from university slang for a private tutor or instructor in sport. Mentoring has its origins in advising and counselling. In the modern business context therefore we can define coaching as being directly concerned with the immediate improvement of performance and development of skills by a form of tutoring or instruction. Mentoring is always at least one step removed and is concerned with the longer-term acquisition and application of skills in a developing career by a form of advising and counselling. Although informality is part of the day-to-day operational reality in many organisations, my own belief is that both coaching and mentoring will be more effective where it is a formal requirement and part of a person's job description. So my definition of mentoring assumes that the role should be formalised by the organisation requiring it.

I have applied these definitions in the research for this book and I believe they stand up well. In the same way that I have identified three main types of coaching roles, the research also established three main types of mentoring role. These are:

- the mainstream Mentor, who is someone who acts as a guide, adviser and counsellor at various stages in someone's career from induction, through formal development to a top management position;
- the professional qualification Mentor, who is someone required by a professional association to be appointed to guide a student through their programme of study, leading to a professional qualification;
- the vocational qualification Mentor, who is someone appointed to guide a candidate through a programme of development and the accumulation and presentation of evidence to prove competence to a standard required for a National Vocational Qualification.

The mainstream Mentor

My definition of a mainstream Mentor is someone who acts as a guide, adviser and counsellor at various stages in someone's career from induction, through formal development to a top management position.

The idea that, as part of the normal induction programme, one person is nominated to look after a new starter is quite commonplace. The tasks usually involve making general introductions, showing the layout of the building, completing essential paperwork and perhaps accompanying the new starter to lunch. These formal responsibilities are often quickly discarded and are rarely termed mentoring.

This practice is changing in some organisations. In both retailers B & Q and Boots the Chemist there are examples of the store manager, supervisor or store trainer extending the role towards an ongoing mentoring relationship. But these individual practices have not yet been formalised into a companywide policy so do not count as examples of mainstream mentoring.

In American Express, where graduate recruits do have Mentors formally appointed, the recruits themselves felt that there was a need for the induction Mentor role. With the agreement of the company, they instituted what they termed the 'buddy' or 'partner' system. This involved each new member of the graduate development programme having a 'partner' appointed from members of the previous programme to act as a friend and adviser. The system was intended to ensure good communications between graduates and to give the newcomer useful insights into the programme and company policies. The system requires the experienced graduate to act as the Mentor or partner and to take responsibility for regular informal meetings with the new graduate – a monthly lunch was suggested. The programme is monitored by the personnel department to ensure that the meetings do take place. This regular but informal access to a more experienced person who will give advice and counsel when requested is the essence of a mentoring relationship.

In ICI Pharmaceuticals, the induction Mentor is a formalised role within the personnel department. The system has been designed and policy guidelines have been issued (see Appendix 5). These guidelines emphasise the learning process the new starter will be experiencing; the care needed in selecting a Mentor and some thoughts on the nature of the relationship, including that of an ongoing sounding board.

Sheila Hyslop was one of the first new starters to experience the mentoring system. After graduating with a geography degree in 1990, Sheila was appointed as a trainee personnel officer with ICI Pharmaceuticals in Macclesfield. The person who sent her the letter offering her the position was actually her future Mentor and he wrote to her in that capacity. Her Mentor was an experienced personnel officer and senior manager two steps up from her manager.

After being introduced to her Mentor in her first few days, Sheila met him weekly. As she became more settled and familiar with her position, meetings became fortnightly and eventually monthly, though this was an arbitrary development – there are no rules on the frequency of meetings.

In their first few meetings, the Mentor took time to introduce her to the company and give her a broad view of longer term career structure, opportunities and expectations. Sheila believes this breadth of view was an important feature of their mentoring relationship as more detailed and day-to-day aspects of her job were covered by her immediate manager. As she became familiar with her job, so Mentor meetings became more and more driven by her. Now, two or three days before each meeting she sends her manager a rough agenda of the things she wants to discuss. Often, as a result of these discussions, the Mentor suggests mini-projects to be attempted before the next meeting.

She now feels free to arrange a meeting at short notice if she has any problems. On one of these occasions she was having trouble in building an effective relationship with another member of staff who was working in her section. She saw her Mentor who guided her to solutions she was able to put into practice immediately. Another time she was preparing for a presentation she had to make. Her Mentor gave her the option to rehearse it before him first.

Sheila sees the Mentor as someone who can help her with a 'major strategic long-term vision' of her career. He keeps her looking forward and broadens her perspectives. She thinks that a good Mentor should be a good listener who is part counsellor and part confidant. Because he works at a different location, she feels she can tell him about any problems she may have with other members of staff.

The experience of the Mentor is important too, Sheila believes. He needs to be senior and experienced enough to see and understand clearly the career route the protégé might take but should not be so senior as to be held in awe.

Strengths and weaknesses of mainstream mentoring

Some of Sheila's observations were reflected in the views of two graduate recruits in North West Water, Anne and John. These new graduates first met their Mentors at the end of their first week at work. They were made to feel that this relationship would be crucial to the successful launch of their careers. They were also told that their Mentors were very senior and successful managers. Needless to say, this did nothing for their nerves and consequently they felt the first meeting was very tense and it had not been held in the best atmosphere. This was subsequently picked up in the review of the induction course. Management development manager Kathleen Johnstone adds: 'This is an example of good intentions backfiring. The stress on the seniority of the Mentors was intended only to highlight the Company's commitment to the trainees – a lesson well learnt and next year we will play it much more low key.'

Meetings thereafter took place at the beginning and end of each work placement and at intervals of a minimum of six weeks. Trainees could also contact their Mentors at other times if required. Each meeting was a chance for the Mentor to check on the trainee's general progress and ensure that the correct amount and variety of work experience was being provided.

As in any one-on-one relationship, the value of mentoring depends very much on the commitment of the individuals involved. One of the two trainees had a 'rather frosty relationship' with his first Mentor. By contrast, the other one got on extremely well and even continued to ask his advice after he had retired.

Of the benefits they thought they had gained from the Mentor, foremost were:

- source of reassurance/backup figure;
- help in lateral thinking and achieving overview of career and organisation;
- driving force to push them if they needed it;
- alternative and detached point of guidance from immediate manager;
- an opportunity to see clearly what skills and experiences they needed;
- chance to learn organisation skills;
- qualified sounding board for any questions or problems they encountered;
- chance to become acquainted with someone much higher up in the company.

Amongst the pitfalls and elements they felt were lacking or could be improved were:

- lack of critical feedback from Mentors;
- difficulty of breaking the ice in the first few weeks – a time they felt they needed an effective Mentor most;
- uncertainty/insecurity as to how much interaction took place between Mentor and line-manager;
- difficulty of airing questions without feeling foolish;
- awe factor – feelings of nervousness and inhibition because of importance, seniority and age-difference of Mentor;
- discomfort of comparing themselves and (they felt) being compared with other protégés;
- the fact that the quality of Mentor seemed so variable and therefore the possibility of envy of someone with a particularly good Mentor.

The practice in NWW of ensuring that programmes are regularly reviewed and the feedback used to adjust future programmes is one I would recommend. Inevitably new mentoring schemes will have to be piloted, and even when firmly established, should have an evaluation process included.

In American Express, the graduate development programme has been running for several years and the formal appointment of a Mentor is an integral part of the programme. Jane Champ is the personnel manager with responsibility for the programme and for selecting the Mentors from among senior management. She explains:

> 'The Mentor has to be in a grandfather position but not directly responsible for the recruit's department. We try to ensure that a graduate will have a director as a Mentor and that MBA recruits have a vice president as Mentor. These Mentors are often very high profile individuals and great care is needed in matching and selecting. The Mentor has to possess coaching and counselling skills and, most importantly, provide a good all round role model.
>
> 'The Mentoring system is not tightly prescribed but monthly meetings are recommended and guidelines are issued to both parties. The "contract" approach of a mutual agreement of what each can deliver is much favoured. The relationships that develop are as varied as the individuals involved.
>
> 'Our Mentors appear to value the role. The programme had high visibility and is sponsored at the highest level. The role gives senior managers a window into the organisation and to broader social issues, from a grass roots level perspective. The talented young people can make for a stimulating relationship and provide a welcome variety in a senior executive's job.'

An important consideration for any organisation embarking on a mentoring system is how they choose their Mentors. Jane summarises the qualities she looks for in a Mentor as someone who:

- treats people as colleagues;
- is on the lookout for opportunities to help people learn;
- makes company norms and philosophy explicit and understandable;
- regularly discusses an individual's career plan and goals;
- wants people to succeed;

- is prepared to free up time to spend with an individual (often at short notice);
- challenges an individual to do their best.

This suits the American Express context but other organisations will have to adjust this profile to their own business and to the range and calibre of senior managers available, willing and capable of filling this role. Defining the role clearly at the outset is another key requirement.

Wider issues

One issue on which most people we talked to in the research phase agreed was that confining mentoring to graduate recruits and selected internal employees heightened division between them and non-graduate members of staff. This is a tricky issue to resolve for organisations thinking of introducing mentoring. Most senior management teams are interested in investing in future managers, many of whom will probably be graduates, but there are always only limited resources available for management development. Also, mentoring is a new and unfamiliar concept and will take time to prove its value. Patience is probably the only realistic answer that can be given to those who would like mentoring to be available to all new starters.

Another lesson to be learned is the danger that protégés who are allocated a Mentor may get their own importance out of perspective. In British Airways, where experienced pilots were appointed to mentor young pilot cadets, one side effect was that some cadets after qualification acted rather as prima donnas. Seasoned pilots and line managers then had the task of bringing them down to earth (no pun intended). This may have been another instance where initial enthusiasm for mentoring led to an overemphasis of the role. In a different company, a secretary pointed to another negative consequence of mentoring graduate recruits. She had to organise the introductory visits for the young graduates and said 'It was like organising a Royal Tour. They acted with such self-importance that it caused us a great deal of resentment.'

These examples highlight the importance of positioning a new mentoring system with great care. Yes, it is important. But so are other activities and other people's aspirations.

Mentoring for senior managers

Another issue that arises is should the senior managers in the organisation have a Mentor appointed to help them? My own experience as a managing director of a company newly acquired by a larger public company was that the non-executive chairman appointed by the new owners played a valuable role. This was helpful in enabling me to understand the developing politics in the new situation. He acted also as a sounding board on new business ideas. My experience as a personnel director, however, was that I had very little time either to be mentored or to act as a Mentor. Day-to-day operational needs meant that acting as a Coach to help improve immediate performance was a higher priority.

As a management consultant I have found the mentoring role develops with the client managers quite often on longer term assignments but rarely on short projects. But one of the most interesting recent developments which combines mentoring and management consultancy comes from a book: *The Goal*.

The Goal is written in a fast-paced thriller style by Eli Goldratt and Jeff Cox. It is an extraordinary blend of novel, leading-edge management theory and the Socratic teaching method. Alex Rogo is a harried plant manager, working ever more desperately to try to improve performance. His factory is rapidly heading for disaster. So is his marriage. He has 90 days to save his plant or it will be closed by corporate HQ, with hundreds of job losses. A chance meeting with a colleague from student days - Jonah - helps Alex break out of conventional ways of thinking to see what needs to be done.

Jonah is described as a Mentor and Goldratt uses this device to demonstrate the power of the Socratic approach to develop deductive reasoning in the learner. As Goldratt puts it: 'Jonah in spite of his knowledge of the solutions, provoked Alex to derive them by supplying the question marks instead of the exclamation marks.'

One consequence of the book's popularity is that it has encouraged the formation of the Theory of Constraints Club with branches now established throughout USA, Europe and Israel. At club meetings Goldratt's logical thinking process is used (and practised) to analyse articles describing dialogues between Jonah and Alex. These dialogues, termed 'late night discussions', concern generic business issues such as transfer pricing and single source vending. The role of the Mentor in the group is to help the club members explore the thinking process to resolve problems, the subject matter being largely immaterial. Group members examine the dialogues in a rigorous 'effect–cause–effect' manner building logic trees of the current situation. This leads to the identification of the core problem. Once this is identified a similar rigorous approach is undertaken with the solution.. As Oded Cohen of the Goldratt Institute so clearly puts it: 'Many of the problems of today are solutions of yesterday'.

This example shows that Mentors can work with groups as well as on a one-to-one basis. This may be a good way to encourage senior managers to adopt the role or a good way to get experienced Mentors to train other senior managers. Certainly the training of Mentors is an issue to be tackled when introducing a new mentoring system.

Apart from recommending also that senior managers read *The Goal* or hire a good Mentor/Consultant, I will leave the senior managers' needs and move on to another well defined mentoring role – the professional qualification Mentor.

The professional qualification Mentor

I have defined this role as someone required by a professional association to be appointed to guide a student through their programme of study, leading to a professional qualification. Many organisations have staff who belong to professional associations and may therefore need to adopt this role. The experiences gained might also be applicable in other situations.

Most professional institutes or associations have strict qualification criteria for eligibility for membership. Most, too, have developed extensive educational programmes to help young people obtain the necessary qualifications. The role of Mentor is often specified as part of the process albeit that sometimes the term is not used explicitly.

Malcolm Berry was one of the first people to become a Mentor at ICI Engineering when the scheme was introduced in the 1970s. The mentoring system was developed as part of the Monitored Professional Development Scheme introduced by the Institution of Mechanical Engineers. It was designed to encourage graduates to aspire to full institutional membership as Chartered Engineers. The Mentor was appointed to guide them through the programme. Malcolm explains his role:

> 'Graduates meet their Mentor in their first few days with the company and will continue to meet every month throughout the four-year programme. The Mentor will preferably be chosen from a field related to the graduates but will almost certainly not be in the same workplace.'

Malcolm's protégés can contact him at any time. He can help them with professional as well as social matters, for example looking for accommodation or settling into a new area. A lot, naturally, depends on the personal relationship struck up between the two.

The Mentor meets the graduate's manager on a regular basis (every three months in Malcolm's case) in order to check that the right amount and correct breadth of experience and training is being achieved. This does not, in Malcolm's opinion, undermine the Mentor's role of confidant should there be any difficulties between graduate and manager.

There is no formal training provided for prospective Mentors. They are appointed on the basis of their experience and briefed as to what their role is. Thereafter things are left very much in the Mentor's control. Malcolm feels that a good Mentor should be first and foremost a role model for the protégé. He should be someone with at least five years' experience at ICI and have plenty of technical experience to deal with any potential work problems. He should be a source of energy and enthusiasm, but must be realistic and fair.

Malcolm got great satisfaction from his role as a Mentor. He found the feedback from young graduates useful and he recognised a definite feeling of pride about people he had mentored. Over a 14-year period they had become like an extended family: 'to some extent you are a bit of a father figure'.

The negative aspects in Malcolm's experience were the chance of the graduate having to stay in one location for an extended part of the four-year training period and hence the feelings of dislike a graduate may have of being compared with other protégés assigned to the same Mentor. He stressed that the Mentor had to be careful in any judgements made over promotions or possible moves.

Malcolm felt that the relationship benefited from being part of the recognised 'professional development' of an engineer sharpening the individual's ability so enabling them to emerge as a professional engineer. The twin focus of the system was 'personal development' – nurturing the individual to assume a full and sensitive role in the community. The Institution emphasises these points by encouraging the Mentor to look on the candidates as their 'charges' not their protégés. This means that criteria for success can be differentiated from judgements made against internal standards. This emphasises the personal career development of the candidate rather than the immediate needs of the organisation.

This example includes another point to bear in mind when introducing mentoring, namely the importance of ensuring that the relationship between the line-manager and the Mentor is clearly explained to both. The line-managers will normally be focused on the organization's immediate needs whereas the Mentor will be taking a longer-term view.

The Institute of Chartered Accountants is another professional body that places obligations on its members to perform a mentoring role as part of the new member's qualification process. They do not use the term Mentor but describe the role as that of Counselling Member. An extract from the Institute's official guide explains the role and this format might act as a framework for other organisations who wish to adopt a succinct policy statement. The guide explains:

> The role of Counselling Members in developing students' professional attitudes is paramount and such members must be selected carefully. The major qualities required are enthusiasm, the ability to motivate young people and a genuine interest in their welfare and development.
>
> Counselling Members need not be experts in all aspects of education and training but it is essential that they are fully aware of:
>
> a) the background and current performance of the students for whom they are responsible;
> b) the current examination structure and overall syllabus;
> c) the timing and main content of any in-house courses;
> d) the office's arrangements for examination tuition and policy on resits.
>
> A lack of knowledge in these areas reduces the Counselling Member's credibility in the eyes of the student and, thereby, lessens the impact of any counselling points made. Similarly, Counselling Members should be seen to have the authority to speak for their office and for this reason should normally be partners.
>
> The responsibility for counselling should be shared between as many partners as possible to ensure that advice is available from a broad platform within the partnership. The ratio of students to Counselling Members should not normally be more than 15:1 so that members have the time to devote to the role and to get to know their students as individuals. Uninformed, unenthusiastic or late counselling is counter-productive.

David Frankel is one of the partners at KPMG Peat Marwick who is responsible for helping partners meet their obligation. He explains that the firm's policy is that while no partner has to become a Counsellor, they are strongly encouraged to do so. Partners are initially paired randomly with students partly because of the large numbers involved and partly 'because accountants are instinctively suspicious of using behaviour methodology to make these sorts of decisions'.

The system is supported with detailed documentation and is part of the overall assessment process described in more detail in Chapter 6. Counselling interviews are held every six months and the topics covered include:

- the matters arising out of the six-monthly appraisal interview with their line managers;
- skills developed over the last six months;
- extent of the individual's satisfaction with their development to date;
- the individual's goals for the next six months;
- longer term career goals;
- skills requirements and training necessary;
- action plan to meet objectives.

In practice David explains the detailed responsibilities of the Counselling Member are delegated to the students' managers who monitor their performance and development closely. The liaison between senior manager and partner allows the system to work 'as well as can be expected with human systems'. David has devised training for partners. Among the issues highlighted by the training are:

- the need to distinguish between appraisal and counselling roles;
- the need to recognise potential problems between young, inexperienced people reacting to, by definition, older and successful partners;
- the need to run interviews in an encouraging and confidence-boosting style.

The Counselling Member role is therefore very similar to that of the Mentor in other professional qualification processes. When asked why accountants did not use the term Mentor, one of the partners of KPMG Peat Marwick replied: 'Well it doesn't sound very British does it? So I suppose we will avoid using it for as long as we can!' This honesty and pragmatism underlines the point I've made about the importance of being able to define the role irrespective of what you call it.

The vocational qualification Mentor

I have defined the vocational qualification Mentor role as someone appointed to guide a candidate through a programme of development and the accumulation and presentation of evidence to prove competence to a standard required for a National Vocational Qualification.

In the area of vocational qualification 'to mentor' has become both a new role as well as a new word in the management dictionary. Let me use three examples to illustrate this development. The first two show the type of advice and guidance that line managers and candidates will receive and have to operate within depending on the awarding body offering the qualification. The third shows how one manufacturing company has implemented the system.

Mentoring for professional bodies

The Institution of Industrial Managers (IIM) is a professional body which has taken a leading role in the implementation of competence-based qualifications for managers. This has meant reshaping some of its well-established education and training programmes and introducing the concept of the company-based Mentor as an essential part of the process they recommend. The Institution explains:

> 'The IIM's three one-year "Leader Series" management development programmes are designed to integrate the students' day-to-day learning opportunities at work with the training given at the "delivery centres" (colleges or other establishments operating the IIM programmes). In these programmes the students are required to demonstrate that they are competent managers by the application of management techniques, wherever possible in a work environment. The programmes are therefore unlike the previous IIM Courses (and many others) that primarily tested students' knowledge and understanding by written examinations.
>
> 'Our IIM programmes require students to have a company Mentor to guide them in the application of what they learn and to give feedback on performance. Modern approaches to learning recognise the amount of development that can occur through "doing" as distinct from "studying". Experience of itself does not however automatically provide learning. Learning only takes place if the development opportunities are identified, the experience gained is reflected upon and the performance evaluated. The Mentor can encourage the students to reflect on and evaluate their performance at work, and can therefore help them learn. The delivery centre tutors, because they cannot have the same full appreciation of the working environment, are only partially able to assist the students to develop their ability in this way.

'The Mentor's function is therefore to complement, not replace, the training and assessment undertaken by the delivery centre. The Mentor should be involved in counselling, facilitating work-based learning and assisting with assessment of the student's ability.

'Mentors are involved in the programme primarily to help the student, but there can be other useful benefits. Delivery centres (and the IIM) get regular feedback from senior managers that enables them to ensure that the training provided continues to meet the real needs of local industries. Some company Mentors have reported that they have personally benefited from the liaison with tutors and students. It also helps to keep tutors fully up to date with the application of modern industrial and commercial practices.'

This explanation by the IIM not only reflects their underlying philosophy but also usefully highlights the changed role of the tutors from local educational institutions. For many organisations vocational qualifications are currently handled in partnership with local education bodies. The introduction of mentoring will require consultation, at least, with current suppliers.

The City and Guilds is an awarding body for many different qualifications. It too has been adjusting its programmes to meet the new competence-based qualification standards. In its guidance to Mentors involved in its retail management qualification programme, it explains why the new Mentor role is necessary for supervisory and management qualifications as opposed to qualifications for basic operatives' functions. City and Guilds define the differences as follows:

1. Supervisors and managers have to exercise the autonomy of their work role which does not lend itself to direct observation assessment methods.
2. Supervisors and management roles are complex, often requiring a large degree of planning and organising.
3. The retail NVQ at these levels is a broad based qualification and varied sources and types of evidence are required to prove competence.

The City and Guilds guidelines continue in an enthusiastic tone:

The onus is placed on candidates to identify and collect their own evidence of competence. Imagine being able to decide all the following things for yourself for a qualification you wished to achieve:

- what evidence will prove competence;
- how much evidence to collect;
- over what period of time evidence should be collected;
- which units to work towards;
- whether to use the help of others.

Some people faced with all these choices may give up fairly easily – some may not start at all. This is where the Mentor comes in. By providing help and support to candidates, Mentors can help them to achieve their goal. The best way to help anyone is to encourage them to help themselves and this really is the nature of the role that the Mentor carries out. [I discuss this in more detail in the skills chapters.] There are a number of stages in the NVQ in which encouragement, advice and support may be welcome. The particular stages are:

- identifying the units and the order of units which candidates should work towards;
- identifying the evidence that is available to candidates;
- agreeing an action plan;
- reviewing progress;
- presenting the evidence.

The similarity between the role of the vocational qualification Mentor and qualifier Coach and that of the Assessment Adviser discussed in the next chapter is striking. Exactly what the role is may appear slightly confusing to outsiders, but the important thing is that it is defined internally within the organisation.

Mentoring in manufacturing

Both IIM and City and Guilds therefore encourage companies to appoint Mentors. Jaguar Cars were one of the first companies to tackle the implementation of competence-based qualifications. As part of this process, they developed a company statement on the role of Mentors which sums up the issues from their perspective:

> In order to assist Jaguar to achieve its objectives and to improve its performance, attention has to be paid to the quality and retention of new and existing staff. Much in-house training and development is required to support such staff and to encourage the appropriate learning environment.
>
> Using existing experienced staff as Mentors is one of the keys to such developments by underpinning the whole learning environment. Their role as industrial mentors is to support and encourage staff in their development, help them to integrate into the company, and where necessary, act as a bridge or link to other departments to obtain additional learning.

> **This role has been somewhat informal in the past but, with the development of competence-based learning programmes, it is becoming more important since such programmes cannot be properly introduced and managed without proper support systems. Mentors, along with portfolios and Accreditation of Prior Learning, are the essential support features within this training and development structure. As this learning environment expands, the use of Mentors is meant to apply across all departments, for all grades/types of staff, and to a variety of newly emerging competence-based awards such as MCI, IIM, and various NVQs.**
>
> **Mentors themselves are not outside this system of competence-based standards, since they will have agreed company standards of performance and may get accreditation of their achievement as competent Mentors. It is recognised that staff undertaking the Mentor role will have development needs and a training/guidance pack has been produced to support them in turn.**
>
> **Being a Mentor can be a limited activity. However, it is important to the Company, to the Mentor and to the learner. All benefit from a learning environment, from giving attention to individual development.**

Les Ratcliffe, the Jaguar training officer, recognises the overlap between this mentoring description and the coaching role but believes that it is the most appropriate description for his company. The thoroughness of the Jaguar approach is reflected in the model standards of performance for Mentors which they have introduced. There are eleven elements, each with their own performance criteria. One of the elements concerns Jaguar's commitment to total quality but another one touches on an important dimension of a mentoring relationship – how to terminate it. In almost all the mentoring roles we have discussed, it can be seen that the relationship will come to an end. This can be because the programme of study or the acquisition of vocational qualifications has been achieved. Equally, it is likely that the need for mentoring from the same Mentor can decline as people develop in their own careers and gain experience. In any event, the need to reduce or end the relationship should be handled with care. Les Ratcliffe's advice would be to use the following checklist:

- acknowledge that the learner has achieved and advanced sufficiently to be exploring new independence and self-direction;
- establish other sources of future support for the learner;
- offer reassurance at a time of possible uncertainty and anxiety;

- stress you are still available to assist but not necessarily as a Mentor 'safety net';
- celebrate the success of the relationship and what has been achieved.

So what does a Mentor do?

As we have seen, mentoring in a formal sense is a relatively new concept with a variety of interpretations. The answer to the question, then, is probably, 'It depends which organisation you are in and what role they want you to play'. I have defined three roles but in time a generic role will almost certainly be defined in the context of a National Vocational Qualification. This role is unlikely to be a full NVQ but will probably be one unit in several different qualifications. Les Ratcliffe at Jaguar has created one model with eleven separate elements, each with their associated performance criteria. My own idea of a future unit might include the following functions:

1. Establish good rapport with protégés.
2. Assess protégés' needs in consultation with other interested and appropriate parties.
3. Enable protégés to produce and sustain an appropriate development plan.
4. Provide counsel and advice to protégés as required.
5. Monitor protégé performance and progress on a regular basis.
6. Provide feedback to protégés which is constructive and encourages them to accept responsibility for their own development.
7. End the mentoring relationship at the appropriate time and in an appropriate manner.

This model, I suggest, contains the core activities from all the mentoring situations I have discussed. It does not prevent any organisation or professional association adding specific responsibilities which they feel are relevant to their needs; but it does emphasise my view that mentoring should always be defined as being at least one step removed from day-to-day management responsibility for the protégé. If Mentors are given too much direct responsibility, it not only tends to confuse other people involved but it works against the relationship developing into the 'wise and trusted counsellor and adviser' role which lies at the heart of mentoring.

Establishing a mentoring system clearly needs great care and consultation. It is unwise to try and impose what too many seasoned managers will see as an unusual and possibly rather threatening new idea. Clear role definition and mutual expectations should be widely understood. Regular monitoring and adjustments will be necessary so new systems should be piloted with care. It will help if the protégés are involved in this process as their experiences and the amount they gain from them are a crucial factor. But a sense of humour will also be helpful to balance the serious purpose of mentoring.

North West Water reviewed their pilot programme and felt that a Mentor's job description should be drawn up to help clarify the role. It was decided that this should be done by the training department who should also involve the graduate recruits who had been protégés. I reproduce the protégé's proposal as a cautionary tale which shows that the desire to consult is not necessarily repaid with gratitude:

Mentor's Job Description

Purpose

To be a fount of knowledge and perfection embodied, while always remaining approachable. Requires the memory of an elephant, the patience of a saint and an unremitting sense of humour.

Responsibility

- To make line management aware that graduates are already capable of operating a photocopier, and do not require training in tea-making.
- To amend training programme so often that it becomes illegible, thereby dodging any criticism for failing to stick to it.
- Allows graduates to moan about people ignoring them or being hostile while on placement (Mentor should be prepared for the possibility that these people may be his/her closest friends). Gives Mentor a chance to get back at the graduate for all the jokes about their age, under the cover of being brutally honest about how they are doing.
- General agony auntie/someone to rant at/shoulder to cry on. Requires Mentor to have nerves of steel and to be absolutely unshockable.
- To make graduate aware of all the unofficial rules of the organisation, and exchange gossip. Enables the Mentor to find out what is going on in the organisation.

- To ensure that all graduates go on at least one course involving clambering over large obstacles in mud carrying a dozen raw eggs.
- To defend the training section from hordes of moaning graduates, and referee the scrum in the event of a dispute.
- To vilify the training programme, while maintaining that your graduates are making excellent progress, unlike any of the others.
- To shield the graduate from any contact with the training department which might give them an opportunity to discuss your performance as a Mentor.

What makes a good Mentor?

Clearly a sense of humour and patience when dealing with new recruits will be an important attribute!

I hope I have given sufficient examples and profiles of the qualities and characteristics of successful Mentors to enable you to draw up your own profile. A profile which suits your own needs is clearly important as it will help in the selection of Mentors. And some form of selection will almost certainly be necessary even if the official policy of your organisation is that all senior managers should become Mentors. Not everyone will be suitable or will want to do it. Explaining the role clearly will help make the selection process as painless as possible.

Most new Mentors will benefit from some form of training even if only to appreciate the expectations and anxieties that their protégés will have. The range of skills that a Coach needs to develop will also be appropriate for a Mentor. Questioning techniques, goal-setting and giving feedback which builds confidence and success are probably the most important. I deal with them in more detail in the skills chapters. As an overall guide, I would suggest the following checklist:

Checklist

1. Understand how mentoring differs from other roles you are asked to play.
2. Only take on the role if you want to do it and are willing to make the necessary time available.
3. Assess your own strengths and weaknesses and relate them to the protégé's development needs so that you can guide them to other sources of help where it is appropriate.
4. Invest time early in the relationship to establish rapport and a regular schedule for discussions.
5. Enable the protégé to produce a realistic development plan and ensure that it is 'signed off' by all the relevant people.
6. Keep the relationship on a professional level particularly where there are differences in gender. Sensitivity to potential misinterpretation in language and behaviour will be important in these situations.
7. Understand the distinction between counselling and advising and whenever possible encourage the protégé to work out their own solutions with you acting only as a sounding board.
8. Remember you will be a role model and that how you are seen to manage in day-to-day situations will affect the relationship you have with the protégé.
9. Feedback you give should be clear, honest and constructive and designed to build confidence and ongoing commitment in the protégé.
10. Recognise when the time has come to end the relationship and aim to end on a positive and supportive note by sharing the benefits you have both gained from the experience.

CHAPTER 6
What Do I Have to Do if I am an Assessor?

The answer to this question is not straightforward. First you have to decide what form of assessment you are involved in.

Assessment, of course, is not a new word in the management vocabulary. Any organisation must ensure that some form of regular assessment of performance takes place. This can range from the annual meeting with your accountant if you are a one-person business, to the verdict at a general election on the performance of a government. At work over the last 20 years, the word assessment has often been synonymous with appraisal schemes. More recently it has been connected also with industrial psychologists, psychometric testing, assessment centres and other state of the art ideas.

I am more concerned with assessment of performance by people who are not psychologists or by people who have the award of a qualification as their main focus. For those who want to know more about assessment centre processes and other psychological techniques, the Institute of Personnel Management have produced a first-class summary in their Fact Sheet series No 22 October 1989. It contains a wealth of information.

It is important to make the distinction between assessing performance in the general sense and the very specific new sense of assessing performance as part of the National Vocational Qualification process. I start with the general Assessor's role and look at examples in nursing, accountancy, pharmaceuticals and electronics. I then turn to the Assessor in the workplace helping people towards vocational qualification with examples from different parts of the retail industry and the water industry. We then look at a very specialist Assessor role for obtaining vocational qualifications by a process of gaining credit for previous experience or attainment (commonly called APL or APA) with examples from four different work situations.

In each of these activities, the underlying knowledge and many of the skills required are very similar. These have been identified over the years by the industrial psychologists as well as experts from business, education and the academic world. Many readers will already have received appropriate training, either in appraising, interviewing or counselling skills or in effective listening and questioning. But as assessing for qualifications becomes more the focus, then some additional training will be essential. Learning how other people have developed Assessor skills in a variety of situations is an important step in understanding what you have to do to become an Assessor.

Developing nurses to be Assessors

Tricia Campbell is a tutor at the Riverside College of Health Studies in London. She considers self-assessment an important part of a nurse's development as a teacher and Assessor. She explains how it fits in to the nurse's development.

Courses are offered at the College, designed for post-registration nurses who spend a lot of their time teaching and supervising (coaching) their junior colleagues on the wards. The courses focus especially on sharpening teaching and assessing skills. Tricia is convinced that the two skills are inseparable and that assessment from various sources is invaluable: 'How can you teach effectively if you can't assess?' Candidates on these courses are taught to assess through defining objectives and then judging outcomes against these objectives through self-, peer- and tutor-assessment. The objectives are expressed as competency statements which specify the criteria laid down for the identification of individual learning needs.

Learning to teach and assess in this context involves learning the theory and practising teaching and assessment of others as well as having regular opportunities for feedback and self-assessment. Each course member is expected to self-assess their personal learning needs at the start of the programme. Then, individual members decide the level of learning they wish to progress to within the course and review these goals with their 'preceptor' (someone on the ward who combines the role of Coach, Mentor, teacher, and Assessor) and course tutor.

Candidates document their work, interactions, interviews, assessments and reflections in a specially designed course member profile document. This serves as their guide, journal and prime self-assessment tool. This profile is a record of the course member's progress and is used to provide evaluations of progress. To make best use of the Profile, the course member must first be able to assess his or her current experience and knowledge of teaching and assessing and then develop a learning contract which allows for development. Once this is agreed, the course member's growth and development can be measured through a combination of self-, peer- and tutor-assessment, all of which is documented.

Members are encouraged to record any relevant experience - an interaction with a patient, a group discussion, a useful lecture, a description of assessment interactions, an observation. It is then up to the member to select what they would like to discuss with their preceptor, tutor or peers, or include in assignments and evaluations. The completed profile, while allowing for continuous assessment, also provides the portfolio of evidence that informs the final assessment at the end of the course.

After completing the course, learners can apply to become Assessors themselves. To do this, they must observe and document two assessments carried out by already registered Assessors and be interviewed by the director of nursing who assesses their observations. Tricia comments:

> 'Practical assessment is inherent in nursing but there is little doubt that this relatively new process of continuing and self-assessment is seen to be growing. The active involvement of the learner in her own assessment is valued as a way of encouraging good teaching. It is welcomed. The move away from the didactic approach of "right and wrong" judgements to continuous formative, summative and holistic assessment is seen as a crucial ingredient of developing nurses as effective Coaches, Mentors and Assessors; a role which, when combined with teaching, we call a preceptor.'

Helping trainee accountants to assess themselves

David Clifford is the national student recruitment partner in charge of recruitment for the multinational accountancy firm KPMG Peat Marwick. David believes the first five years' experience of work are crucial in the development of highly competent and qualified accountants. His firm, like most accountancy firms, has traditionally paid great attention to the training of young graduates. David explains that recently:

> 'we reviewed how we were doing this throughout the firm. We found that there were many different examples of excellent practice and some pockets where it could be improved. We decided we would draw together best practice into a single process we call the career planning document. We give it to new graduate recruits to use themselves to prepare for their one-to-one sessions with their counselling partner (Mentor) which take place every six months.'

The document spells out KPMG Peat Marwick's philosophy as well as suggesting a step-by-step process. The planner is an excellent example of best practice and an edited version is included in Appendix 2 (see page 158).

The career planner is a very well-produced document and is designed to be used to record and plan the whole first five years of work experience. The planner contains 17 questions organised under four main headings:

- Where am I now and how have I progressed?
- How do I want to develop?
- What opportunities are available?
- How could I get there?

The detailed questions are carefully thought out and phrased to cover the four phases of career development. Students are encouraged to consider all of them each time they review their progress, and also the key issues they would like to raise at their next interview with their counselling partner (Mentor).

Two years after its introduction, David Clifford concedes that he has learnt some lessons which would modify his approach. He explains:

> 'The planner is absolutely right as a statement of where we believe we should be in the process of self-assessment of developing competence and personal awareness. But we probably tried to get there in one big leap rather than step by step. All of us are inclined to be a bit lazy about planning for ourselves and some students have certainly found a five-year planner difficult to "buy into". Of course, without ownership, self-assessment processes don't work too well. Individual six-month or annual planners would be more manageable. So too would fewer questions in the early years. We also have to accept that busy partners sometimes have not given the required time to encourage students

to make best use of the planner. But we are making progress and increasingly it will become part of the culture of the firm.'

Well-designed documentation

Both the nursing and the accountancy approach stress the responsibility of the individual to assess themselves and to use their management structure to gain feedback. In both instances, the organisation provides a process and guidance in the documentation they provide.

'Not *more* complicated forms to fill in!' was often the complaint of busy line-managers in industry when appraisal schemes were first introduced. The clear and careful design of the paperwork, which is an essential ingredient in any assessment system, is very important. Trying to cram too much information onto too small a form is a recipe for the system to be discredited. Clear explanation of the purpose and process to be followed is another essential. But more important perhaps is the relevance and benefit of the assessment to the job that the individual and their manager are expected to do.

Assessing against performance standards

The concept of assessment being linked to clear performance standards, rather than vague comments like 'overall performance satisfactory', has gained ground. Many organisations have introduced new performance review systems to replace their original appraisal schemes with the performance standards framed to suit their own business needs.

There are broadly two approaches that are followed. The first can be classified as 'open-ended' where the manager has to define the performance criteria with the individual concerned and has considerable freedom in how to rate performance. The other approach can be classified as 'structured'. Here the performance criteria are defined by the organisation and so are the ratings to be used in the assessment.

Both approaches have their strengths and weaknesses. The open-ended approach encourages the manager to phrase the required performance standards in specific terms related to targets the individual has to achieve. Unfortunately, many managers find difficulty in writing clear objectives and what ends up on the form is often simply an abbreviated note of the discussion that took place. The 'structured' approach gives little freedom to the people involved but is closer to the organisation's own view of what is required. With this approach the top management have a technique which focusses everyone's attention on specific behaviour and performance outcomes. This can be very useful, particularly if the top management are trying to achieve a culture change in the organisation. Some people however react negatively to the structured 'ticking boxes' approach as an appropriate way to assess their performance, believing that it can be too impersonal and generalist. Many agree, however, that standards-related performance reviews are a great improvement on traditional appraisal schemes.

Examples of the open-ended approach and the structured approach can be seen from ICI Pharmaceuticals and Philips Components respectively (see Appendixes 3 and 4). Both have in common the provision of written guidance for employee and manager which reflects their different approaches. ICI use short bullet-point hints and tips whereas Philips explain in detailed text. In addition to the written guidance managers receive training, and in ICI's case, help with the structuring of objectives and targets.

These two examples give a flavour of the different approaches. The important thing to remember is that both reflect the organisation's view of its own needs. Considerable time and effort has been spent devising these processes and in getting them accepted. Still more will be required to implement them successfully under the day-to-day pressures of work. The suggestion that these schemes should be revamped yet again to take account of national standards devised by an outside body will inevitably face resistance. But this is exactly what is going to be required during the early 1990s.

Assessing for qualifications

The concept of performance standards is fundamental to the National Vocational Qualification movement to provide qualifications based on what people can do rather than solely on their ability to pass exams.

One consequence of changing from an academic and exam-based process to an assessment of performance against strict and tightly defined performance criteria is that someone has to assess people as they 'do it', not just once but consistently enough to be rated competent. The only people who are in a position to make this kind of assessment are an individual's supervisor, manager or specialist colleagues. It is estimated by the NCVQ that 'hundreds of thousands of people will need to be trained as Assessors'. This huge extra workload will not be accepted easily or quickly. But it is inevitable in one form or another.

Same process, different approaches

Every candidate in every organisation is faced with the same basic qualification process. An NVQ is made up of a number of units. Each unit is made up of a cluster of related functions called elements. Each element has a number of performance criteria that have to be met to prove competence. For each element there is also usually a statement on the range of situations in which the competence must be able to be applied. Also included is an indication of the underpinning knowledge required and the typical sources of evidence that might be presented to prove competence.

Each candidate has to produce evidence that they are capable of doing the task consistently. The Assessor's role is to pass judgement on that evidence. The comparison with a law court, lawyers and judges is quite appropriate. But the responsibility for providing the evidence lies squarely with the candidate. This new responsibility will take time to be understood and accepted. Candidates will no longer be fed with knowledge and skills to memorise and regurgitate in examinations held by education and training institutions. They will have to discover, develop it and present their case themselves.

Some candidates will simply have the new process explained to them and be left to fend for themselves until they meet their workplace-based Assessor. But organisations that decide to accept a responsibility to help the candidate through the process will have to decide how to fill the roles of Coach, Mentor and Assessor. Each has a distinctive part to play but each organisation may approach the problem differently.

Some organisations have been introducing the new approach for some time. The national DIY retail chain, B & Q, have introduced a retail NVQ awarded jointly by City and Guilds and the National Retail Training Council. Many of their store staff have already gained store-operative level certificates. To achieve this B & Q have trained and continue to train supervisors as both Assessors and Coaches. North West Water have to train hundreds of operatives to the new NVQ level and are initially using their training instructors. Boots the Chemist have introduced a supervisory management qualification level initially for 400 supervisors out of 1,800. They too are using their training staff and store managers. B & Q have also begun to introduce supervisor and manager qualifications and are training their store managers as Assessors. I examine each company's experience in some detail.

How B & Q assess NVQs

B & Q enthusiastically support the need for a career in retail management. They see the NVQ approach as an ideal way of providing new recruits and existing staff with the opportunity to become appropriately qualified. Translating this policy into day-to-day reality has been a major undertaking. Although taking an NVQ for basic store-operative competencies is not yet mandatory in B & Q, all staff at the appropriate level are offered the opportunity.

B & Q decided to become a City and Guilds approved centre and therefore had to demonstrate that it had the required organisational structure to support its ability to assess the award to City and Guild standards. The regional personnel and training staff play a key role, including that of acting as internal verifiers to ensure that assessments are correctly and consistently being administered. In addition to training supervisors in their role as Coaches and Assessors, in-store trainers coordinate the programme as well as acting as Coach and Assessor. Christine Beresford fills this role in the Southampton store. She explains her role:

> 'Once the trainees have volunteered and been selected to become NVQ candidates, my first task is to explain the NVQ system to them and take them through the introductory guide. I then meet each candidate individually and later with their department manager, to discover, as far as possible, the extent of their existing competencies. Clearly, there will sometimes be elements of competence, particularly at the basic levels, which the candidates already have through previous experience. We have to be able to judge the evidence for this very carefully.
>
> 'Those elements which the candidate is not already competent in will then form a type of checklist for us to work on. Both the candidate's supervisor or manager and I tend to employ a decidedly hands-on method of coaching, showing and telling the candidate what to do and watching and correcting their attempts. I

would describe this as filling in the gaps and adding in the details.

'Each element is assessed when we all feel the candidate is ready. The assessment is done by me but because I am not yet a qualified Assessor (though I hope to be soon) I am observed while assessing by the personnel and training officer. In effect, this means that I am being assessed in order to become an approved Assessor, while carrying out assessments of others. When I feel the candidate has reached the required standard (the terms "pass" or "fail" are never used) then that element has been achieved and can be ticked off.'

The B & Q process is highly structured and very disciplined. Every performance criteria for every element has to be observed, judged, ticked off and recorded. Any laxness is quickly spotted by the personnel and training officer who fulfils a countersigning officer's role and who in turn is subject to scrutiny by a City and Guilds verifier. Myra Ashworth, the B & Q national manager for vocational awards, explains:

'There are two main reasons underlying our approach. The first reflects our desire to achieve a high quality of service for our customers that can be assured if we stick firmly to the performance criteria laid down. The second reflects our determination that retail qualifications should have real status and credibility. Even the slightest departure from the national standards tends to undermine this and that we cannot tolerate. We also have to have regard for the practical realities of our business. Qualifications are important but so too is the efficient and profitable operation of our stores. Combining the role of management supervisor, Coach and Assessor makes operational sense. The supervisor in the workplace is best placed not only to judge competent performance but also to help develop it. Our training staff in turn have a dual role to act as Advisers to the supervisors, and to verify that they are implementing the process properly.'

Assessing supervisors for NVQs

Like B & Q, Boots the Chemist are another pioneer of retail NVQs. They are a larger organisation than B & Q, with around 250 large stores and 800 small stores. With the store-operative level NVQ, Boots followed a process not too dissimilar to that of B & Q; but with the introduction of the supervisory NVQ, the two companies adopted somewhat different approaches.

Both companies faced the same distinction between qualifications for basic functions at store-operative level and the less tangible but equally real functions and performance criteria involved in supervising people for supervisor qualifications. For the basic functions, observation opportunities in the workplace are relatively easy to organise and assess. With supervision, and much more so with management functions, the opportunities are less frequent and do not always produce sufficient or conclusive evidence. The need to rely on additional and different types of evidence from several sources therefore becomes necessary. The timescale involved in building up a portfolio of evidence can be considerable – 9 months might be the shortest with 18 months being the maximum.

The variety of supervisory and management functions for which evidence must be produced is also larger. Although a candidate will be generating evidence naturally through their everyday activities on the job, this focus can lead to conflicts between the candidate's day-to-day responsibilities and their qualification objectives. Understanding, support and advice from the store managers and district managers becomes a crucial factor. This advisory and coaching role is not easily combined with that of Assessor, where objectivity and impartiality are at a premium. This potential clash of roles is not easy to avoid because, operationally, the store manager is the most conveniently located person to do the assessing and appears to be the most appropriate person.

Both organisations intend to tackle these issues through additional training and by ensuring wherever possible that an Assessor does not assess a candidate they have directly coached. (It is worth noting that other organisations, like North West Water, intend to use external Assessors rather than internal managers in this role. NWW believe their culture would not easily absorb the conflicts of interest between Coach, Adviser and Assessor.)

B & Q extended their store operative approach to the supervisor and manager level with an initial programme in 2 of the company's 20 districts. In both of these, a number of experienced store managers and assistant managers were selected to act as Assessors and received several days' training to be able to advise and assess to the new standards. Initially too, the candidates and all managers also received training to ensure that they understood the requirements. For many of the managers, the training was the first detailed exposure to the NVQ process. The difficulty they would feel in adapting their normal 'can-do problem solving' operational management style to that of Coach, Adviser and Assessor was recognised. Great attention was paid to designing the training to suit the culture changes implied. For the Assessors, use was made of role-playing the new situations that they would face and the skills they would need to demonstrate, focussing particularly on the need for constructive encouraging feedback and the motivational aspects of the Assessor's role. In addition, the training covered the assessment process, the evaluation of evidence and the effective use of observation and questioning. After the training was evaluated, it was used to prepare other supervisors and managers in the company.

Developing Assessors in Boots the Chemist

Boots the Chemist faced a somewhat different situation as Lisa Owen, the person in Boots responsible for the implementation of the supervisor-level NVQ, explains:

> 'Initially we identified 400 candidates for supervisor level out of a potential of nearly 1,800. In fact many of these candidates had been Assessors for store operatives and were therefore familiar with the language and processes. They also realised how much time and commitment was needed from themselves and their line managers but that, ultimately, the onus was on them to produce the evidence.'

Boots already had well-developed supervisory and management development programmes. Some supervisors were also selected to study for a National Examination Board supervisory skills qualification. Boots therefore decided to build on their existing programmes and design a new course to meet the new requirements. Lisa explains:

> 'Training of Assessors varies between one and two days dependent on the knowledge and skill of the Assessors. For small stores, where the absence of the pharmacist who is usually the manager, can cause serious operational difficulties, a one-day course will be used. Large stores may build in more role plays and take a more flexible approach to the training.
>
> 'It was estimated that approximately 300 line managers would initially be needed to be trained as Assessors to handle the 400

candidates. When the store-operative level was first introduced, a blanket approach to training Assessors was adopted but found to be wasteful. If a supervisor had nobody to assess immediately after the training, a refresher course was needed when the supervisor was required to work with a candidate. As a result, Assessor training for store operatives is an ongoing process, built into the supervisors' development programme.

'It is intended that the same groups will be maintained for every module to enable inter-store relations to develop. Supervisors are encouraged to network with other supervisors and provide a self-support system. Some work outputs from the workshops may be used as evidence for the NVQ, eg the training session plan which is developed for the second day of the training skills module. There are also work-based assignments. Most are designed to relate to two units of competence at a time. Although assignment work can supply some evidence, it is more likely that it will lead to places where most evidence can be gained, eg accident procedure training will lead to correct completion of the accident book. Assignments also form part of the candidate's personal development folder.

'Assessors plan individual assessment programmes with candidates, ideally to coincide with relevant skills workshops. The Assessors act in an advisory and a judgemental capacity. This also reflects the way Boots encourage their managers to behave in non-assessing situations. The reality, especially in small stores, of getting somebody else to carry out the assessment poses real logistical problems. We therefore have to combine the roles.'

Lisa stressed that the assessment process should not be divorced from everyday activities: 'Candidates must get their minds into gear to think constantly of providing evidence of competence. They are encouraged to make diary entries at the end of each day.'

Lisa believes there are three main benefits from the assessment process:

1. Motivation of the supervisors; in the past they have seen all the attention given to the development of YT trainees, and then to employees going through NVQ store-operative level, and now they are enthusiastic to be able to gain recognition for themselves.
2. We are expecting performance levels to rise as a result of

undertaking the qualifications and therefore they will be eligible for better rewards under the performance-related pay scheme.

3. Mutual trust; relationships are building between line-managers and supervisors because they have to sit down and talk to each other on a regular basis. We tended not to be very good at giving feedback on an ad hoc basis.

Lisa concludes: 'There is a great deal of work involved and we accept that it is an ongoing process but it makes us proud to know we are at the cutting edge and helping to set the pace within the industry.'

Assessing water engineers

North West Water started operating at basic levels in a 'controlled' way from the spring of 1992. At the time of writing, not all the necessary standards for the water industry have been finalised, but preparations are in hand at NWW to start on a water distribution NVQ as soon as the company agrees to go ahead. Training and assessment for NVQ Level 2 in mainlaying and servicelaying will be the starting point, followed by other specific areas such as water supply and disposal.

Initially, some 100 candidates will be entered for NVQs and four instructors will be trained as Assessors. As standards in other specialisms are finalised so more instructors will be trained as Assessors and more candidates will be trained and assessed. Eventually it is estimated that 10 instructors and 250 candidates will be involved. Later, non-instructors will have to take on the assessing role. The instructors will be trained in-house as Assessors by their training and development manager who has himself been trained and is now a Water Services Industry licensed Assessor. This approach mirrors that of many other industries but differs from NWW's own approach to management NVQs where external Assessors will be used.

Potential Assessors attend a three-day course which includes an introduction to NVQs; relevant standards, units and elements for the appropriate water specialisms; assessment administration procedures developed for the industry; testing facilities and procedures. Assessors are given considerable opportunity to practise assessing through simulated situations in the training rooms, where most of the real assessing will later take place. Assessors will be responsible not only for judging performance but also for providing appropriate conditions, environment, materials and tools for the performance of the task. Assessors have to prepare job sheets for the assessed tasks and then complete specially prepared assessment checklists for record-keeping.

Assessment for basic-level NVQs in this industry is still based on tests although the NCVQ are keen to eliminate them. Competence will be judged by Assessors observing candidates performing certain tasks which the Assessors have set up according to procedures laid down. Assessors will then have to judge each candidate as passed (competent) or failed (not competent). Assessors will also administer written tests and/or ask a series of suggested questions to check the candidate's knowledge and understanding where necessary.

As a matter of policy agreed with the Water Industry Lead Body assessing is done in the 'controlled environment' of the training centre and not on the job. There are several reasons:

- NWW want training and assessing to be linked and part of the same process, so it is best to assess as part of a training course.
- In theory, all the assessing could be done on the job, but geographically it makes practical sense to have candidates come to the Assessors rather than the other way round. Candidates are otherwise spread all over the North West and it would not make sense to have the Assessors on the road all the time, especially as all the Assessors are themselves instructors.
- The training centre is weather-proof and avoids the possibility that outside on-the-job assessments could be disrupted by bad weather.
- All the assessable tasks at the basic levels lend themselves to being simulated in the training centre, so controlling training and assessment in one place is not seen as a problem in the industry. It was felt that competence could be extrapolated from the weather-proof environment to outside with no problem.

Assessment of prior learning (APL)

Historically one of the main obstacles to people becoming qualified was the need to attend a course at a college or enrol on a study programme with a professional body. The practicalities and timescales involved often meant that people found it difficult to complete the programme, let alone sit and pass the exam. For people with busy jobs, whether at work or at home, or for those who were unemployed or disabled, the qualification system seemed often to work against them, not for them. The result is that there are many people who are efficiently and professionally able to carry out jobs but who have no formal qualifications to prove that they can do so. The NVQ system of crediting prior learning provides an opportunity to tackle this problem and for some is one of the main attractions of the new approach.

As we have seen, all candidates for an NVQ face the same process. To earn a qualification, the candidate has to present a portfolio of evidence to an Assessor to prove that they are currently capable of performing a range of functions to clear-cut performance standards. How, when or why the candidate obtains the evidence does not matter. No specific course or study programme is required. The Assessor will simply judge the evidence presented as proving competence or not.

All NVQs are made up of a number of separate units and a candidate can be assessed and credited one unit at a time. The system of credits allows candidates to build up their qualification at a time and pace that suits their work or domestic situations. It also allows a 'pick and mix' approach. For some units, a candidate may be able to produce evidence of prior experience. For others, a training programme may be needed or enrolment on a study programme with a local college for a specific subject.

Management qualifications

The APL process applies to all NVQs, but one area that it has been particularly applied to is that of management. The issue of management qualifications has been extensively debated for many years. An often bewildering number of qualifications have been available ranging from MBAs to certificates of varying types from different business schools and colleges. Professional bodies like the Institute of Personnel Management, the Institute of Industrial Managers and indeed, as we have seen, the retail industry, all offer specific, but different, courses. In the mid-1980s, dissatisfaction with this situation and a perceived national weakness in the quality of British management led to a major initiative to tackle the problem. All the major management and business institutions, the government and many leading companies came together and launched the Management Charter Initiative (MCI). The main aim was to draw up national standards for overall management qualifications. The MCI have produced two qualifications to date, the Certificate and the Diploma. Both of these sets of standards have been approved by the NCVQ and all the major awarding bodies have agreed to adjust their qualification to the common format. It is a major achievement that, from 1992 onwards, whichever institution you enrol with, they will be able to offer you the opportunity to work for a standard qualification.

The initial trials

North West Water have been particularly interested in these developments. They are a relatively large organisation employing 5,600 people. They have a well-defined programme for professional and graduate recruits' management development, but they also recognise that many of their existing staff and supervisors could take advantage of the new opportunities to become qualified. Kathleen Johnstone, their management development manager, explains:

> 'We were so keen that we volunteered to become involved in the earliest programmes when everyone was working out how this new approach would work in practice. We certainly learned some important lessons from the trials and now have a clear vision of APL's role in our overall development plan.'

Angela and Norma, both from the finance department in NWW, were members of a group that took part in the early programme in order to gain an MCI-level Certificate. At the time, they were relatively new to first-line management. The programme began with a workshop which left them rather bewildered and believing that it was far above their level. They were persuaded to attend the next meeting to give it another chance. This gave them a much clearer understanding of what was expected of them.

Each candidate was then provided with the performance standards divided into nine units. Angela and Norma did not understand clearly that evidence was needed for all nine units before the final certificate could be awarded. This caused difficulty for some candidates as they were unable to provide evidence from prior experience for more than five or six of the units. At the end of the process, therefore, Norma was left with only a partial qualification and felt disappointed.

Once they had been given the list of competencies, the candidates were left with the responsibility of compiling the evidence on their own. Candidates were given a telephone number of an external Adviser they could contact for help but they were reluctant to do so and did not take much advantage of this facility.

After seven months of finding and compiling relevant evidence, the candidates were given a date by which the evidence was to be collected for assessment. Two weeks later, each candidate was invited to a one-to-one meeting with the Assessor to check that all the evidence submitted was their own work. They were then questioned to ensure they fully understood the subjects. If all nine units had been completed to the satisfaction of the Assessor, then a Certificate of Attainment was awarded.

Surprisingly perhaps, it was Norma, the candidate who had insufficient evidence to complete all the units, who felt she got the most out of the experience. This seems to be because she was so new and inexperienced that the programme was relevant to her current development rather than to any previous learning. The process of collecting evidence meant she was forced to get a clear overview of what she was doing while she was doing it. Consequently she believes that the whole process developed both herself and her ability to do her job.

Angela, who had the experience to complete it fully and for whom one might have thought an APL process would have been more relevant, in fact found it rather tedious and repetitive. She found motivation difficult and felt the need for more guidance and advice. While recognising value in having her past learning accredited, she did not feel the process helped her develop further.

A modified approach

Out of the nine candidates who formed the initial group, two were able to complete all nine units and five were able to complete five or six. Kathleen Johnstone comments:

> 'In fact nearly half the candidates from the early group have already been promoted and, looked at dispassionately, they have all benefited. I think we learned three main lessons:
>
> - the candidates need a great deal of support; the process is no easy option and places on the candidate a great deal of responsibility for completing the programme, which they are often unaccustomed to;
> - the APL route is not possible without total involvement and support from line-managers as Advisers and Coaches. I would go as far as saying that if this is unlikely to be forthcoming I would recommend an alternative route to the candidate;
> - we need to relate the process and the standards more closely to our operational and development needs and to the candidate's own development perceptions; we can't

allow APL to exist in some sort of "vacuum of good intentions".'

As a result of their experience, NWW are developing a phased approach to gaining benefit from the APL process. Their plan envisages:

Phase I (6–8 weeks)

a) Relate MCI standards to existing NWW performance standards, identify gaps and differences and develop explanations which managers and candidates can understand and accept.
b) Review existing training programmes against potential candidates' needs; identify any gaps and plan how they might be met if a candidate requested specific help.
c) Identify potential candidates; meet them and their line-manager to explore practical issues, eg timescales, commitment required and level of coaching and mentoring support needed and available.

Phase II (4 weeks)

a) Invite all interested candidates and line-managers to two-hour briefing session (held at end of the day to minimise disruption to normal work). Outline APL process, NVQ standards, timescales and support involved.
b) Invite nominees and volunteers to half-day briefing session at the end of which candidate and line-manager 'sign up' to the programme. Maximum of 10 candidates for Certificate programme and 10 for Diploma. Thus, with line-managers, between 35 and 40 people on programme.
c) Managers attend one-day coaching and mentoring seminar. This is followed by a one-day assessment seminar for line-managers and candidates jointly to ensure mutual understanding of issues and expectations. At the end of the assessment seminar an adviser is appointed to work with each line-manager primarily as support in their role of helping the candidate through the process.

Phase III (36–40 weeks)

a) Line-managers and candidates, or small groups of candidates following an identical programme, review candidate's existing experience against the standards of the unit(s) for which qualification is sought. The outcome is a development plan for the candidate(s) to produce the evidence for their portfolio. Advisers are available as required for specialist support.

b) Candidate(s) complete development plan. This may involve special training and development activities as well as collecting evidence from current and previous work experience. The line-manager and Adviser are available for support as required. Candidates can work individually or in small action-learning groups as required.
c) Candidate(s) present portfolios to external Assessors as and when appropriate. If assessed as competent, candidates repeat the process until all units have been assessed as competent when qualification will be awarded.
d) Line-manager, Advisers, management development staff meet periodically to review progress and identify any additional help and support required for the line-manager or candidate(s). External verifiers from the awarding bodies are included in these review meetings as appropriate.

Phase IV (after 12 months)

a) Full evaluation of programme, including relevance to operational priorities and budget implications.
b) Revised programme, as necessary, launched for next 12 month period.

APL in smaller organisations or for individuals

North West Water are typical of those organisations who have the need, the will and the resources to devote to developing their management potential. Not all organisations will be able to or would readily choose to follow this route. Economics will play a large part but so too will practicalities. Some organisations will be too small to support or need a large programme. Inevitably some candidates will face the prospect of having to work through the process on their own. Those who are unemployed, disabled or thinking of returning to work will face a similar challenge. Access to an external Assessment Adviser will be crucial for this type of candidate, either from a local college or independent delivery centre.

Keith Walton is a management consultant with considerable experience in assessment, developing competencies and running development programmes. In order to become a qualified Assessor, Keith had to assess others and help them to collect their evidence. At the same time, he had to compile records of his own work so that he too could be assessed and accredited. Keith's work is primarily on a one-to-one basis with candidates in quite different occupational environments. His role is therefore that of Adviser, Coach and Assessor.

One of the candidates with whom Keith worked is a staff training and development officer in the National Health Service who planned to achieve two units over a period of three to four months. Keith met with him monthly for at least half a day. During each meeting, progress was reviewed and assessed against the standards, further work or collection of existing evidence agreed and an action plan for the next stage confirmed. Advice was given on how to compile a portfolio, how to identify inserts, relate them to the performance criteria and cross-reference them as necessary. But it was the candidate who took responsibility for doing all this. The candidate commented:

> 'For the lone candidate like me the combination of advisory and assessment roles in my Assessor was crucial. A person who is starting needs an Adviser for the first couple of units and then can be self-operational. That help is especially necessary for understanding the standards and interpreting the precise words. Important too is the personal support provided by the Assessor. There is a need for the candidate to get a boost. I'm not sure I would have felt encouraged to carry on if I had not met regularly with Keith. At the end I was able to say "I've done it" which was a significantly different feeling to "I've passed the exam"!'

One of Keith's main tasks is to help candidates understand the precise wording of each performance criterion of the units. He does this through skilful questioning and probing so that candidates can suggest ways of using, locating, acquiring or developing the evidence needed to satisfy that criterion. Keith believes that it is necessary constantly to see what is realistic within a candidate's organisation and job constraints and how this can be married to and be seen to support the performance criteria. As an Assessor and Adviser, Keith sometimes has to encourage candidates to see 'tasks' as developmental – things that could be done now to satisfy the criteria and which will later prove useful to them and their department. Keith comments: 'The problem with APL is that some performance criteria do not lend themselves easily to certain organisational cultures, therefore if it is not part of the candidate's experience, you've got to persuade them to start to do it.'

Once evidence is produced and clearly explained through a personal statement or report by the candidate, Keith effectively replaces his Adviser's hat with that of an Assessor and judges whether the evidence supports the standard. The candidate is encouraged to see how the evidence might be judged by another Assessor by asking: Does the evidence speak for itself? Is it clear how it matches the standards? Can I reasonably infer from the evidence that the performance criteria are being met?

Keith's continuous involvement and eventual assessment is then verified and formalised by a final assessment panel of fellow Assessors who check for reliability and consistency of assessment.

Sue Edwards, another external Assessor, is a training consultant. She worked with Madeline, a candidate working for the RSA award for the Design and Delivery of Flexible and Open Learning.

Meetings were on a one-to-one basis, with monthly assessment visits, interspersed by evidence accumulation by the candidate. The award (based on successful completion of 6 units out of a total of 30) took six months to complete. The Assessor and candidate spent six days together, mainly devoted to observing Madeline at work. There was also a half-day final assessment of the portfolio by Sue. A panel of peer Assessors then reviewed the portfolio at the end and briefly interviewed the candidate to test, where necessary, her knowledge and understanding.

Sue's role was formally described as that of workplace Assessor. But this entailed also advising the candidate on how to compile her portfolio, reviewing the evidence and helping to relate it to the performance criteria. Assessment involved observing the candidate at work, reviewing peers' observations of the candidate at work and forming judgements on the basis of these observations. Several candidates from the same workplace were working towards the award and they coached each other by observing each other at work and writing narratives of their observations for the Assessor to review. This relieved Sue from this role and she was able to remain more detached, although a close relationship with the candidate inevitably developed.

From Madeline's point of view, the most helpful aspects of the Assessor's role were

> 'clarifying *what* I was doing and being told that I was doing it OK. Sue's initial role in reviewing what I actually did as part of my work and agreeing how that might map on to the standards

> was invaluable. I did not feel very confident initially with the units as they were difficult to understand. I had to get Sue's confirmation and then I could work to produce the evidence.'

Kay Williams is the chief executive of North Devon Manufacturers' Association Training Limited – an organisation set up to cater mainly for the training needs of the young employees of its business members. Having left school only with some O-levels, but having risen to a senior position, Kay took a conscious decision to gain a management qualification through a competence-based approach. In late 1989, as part of the MCI pilot, the Cornwall and Devon Accredited Centre launched a management development programme. Most of those participating were managing government training schemes (eg YTS).

After a briefing day and a two-day residential weekend during which Advisers were chosen and short seminars on various management topics were run, the programme continued as follows:

1. A workplace visit when the appointed Adviser visited Kay to help complete a self-analysis questionnaire and produce a development plan.
2. Monthly individual tutorial visits for portfolio development and coaching sessions.
3. Training when Kay attended a number of short courses on IT, interviewing, etc which she identified as necessary to fill in the gaps and to help finalise her portfolio of evidence.
4. Assessment by a panel of Assessors.

What attracted Kay to this qualification route was that it was job related and did not rely on taking exams:

> 'It could be carried out while continuing to work and it was not a strict classroom syllabus so I could learn and develop on the go. It acted also as a long-term self-development where I could measure my achievement as I went.'

The Adviser's role was very important to Kay who admitted she wanted much reassurance and someone to help check whether a piece of evidence was good enough or sufficient in scope. The Adviser then needed to be confident enough to indicate if the evidence was adequate. The first panel assessment was not a happy experience for Kay. Some 12 months after starting out on the first level of the programme, Kay was ready to submit her complete portfolio for all units. After reviewing her portfolio, the panel 'grilled me' on various pieces of evidence as if it was an academic dissertation but then told me that only a

Record of Achievement could be awarded as the course was not yet accredited. (Since the pilot, the process has been refined and national certification is now available.)

Despite her first disappointing encounter with assessment, Kay continued on to the Diploma and presented her portfolio in April 1991 for certification, this time by the Institution of Industrial Managers who judged her competent after a thoughtful and thorough assessment. The rewards of perseverance for Kay are tangible. She comments: 'Although it took 18 months of hard work, it's given me belief in myself. It's a demonstration of my own achievement.'

So what is the role of an Assessor?

Let's return to our original distinction between assessing performance in the general sense and assessing to help people obtain a vocational qualification. Clearly, from the examples we have discussed, the roles will vary.

For those required to be Assessors of performance in the general sense, there are four key issues:

- the type of assessment job you are being asked to do;
- the processes and documentation you have to use;
- the performance criteria that the organisation has laid down or expects you to define; and
- the help and support available from the organisation.

As the answers will be specific to every organisation, it is not possible to define this type of role in any greater detail.

For those involved in assessing to help people obtain vocational qualifications the roles can certainly be specified in more detail. Experience shows that there are three types of workplace Assessor. One operates almost entirely in the workplace and is termed the first-line Assessor. The second type has to consider evidence from several sources, including sometimes from first-line Assessors. This type is termed the second-line, or specialist, Assessor. The third is involved in the APL process and may be called an Assessment Adviser.

The Assessors' roles can be described in terms of performance standards. These have been the subject of intense public consultation and discussion. These standards are now a unit approved by the NCVQ and can themselves form part of another NVQ award for managers, trainers or specialists.

THE ASSESSOR'S ROLES
All Assessors

1. Explain the assessment processes and the required performance standards and criteria.
2. Recognise competent performance of required standards.
3. Make assessment decision and provide feedback.
4. Explain the Health and Safety, Equal Opportunities and Employment Law and Special Needs issues relating to assessment.

First-line workplace Assessors

5. Identify opportunities in the workplace to collect appropriate evidence of performance.
6. Collect and judge performance evidence against criteria.
7. Collect and judge evidence to support the inference of competent performance.

Second-line workplace Assessors

8. Determine the variety of sources of evidence to be used.
9. Collate and evaluate evidence from different sources.

Assessment Adviser

10. Help candidates identify current areas of competence.
11. Help candidates to collect evidence for assessment.
12. Help candidates to present evidence of assessment.

To gain credit for this unit, it will be necessary to receive basic training followed by considerable practice so that a portfolio of evidence of your competence to assess can itself be assessed. Initially, in the absence of sufficient qualified Assessors, the assessment may well be carried out by experienced people who have received the basic training only. Awarding bodies will need to be satisfied that the quality assurance aspects of assessment are adequate. This will require your organisation, or the external provider, to have the appropriate administration systems including an internal verifier to check individual Assessor's work. Awarding bodies will want to monitor the process regularly and will appoint an external verifier to do the job. The roles of coordinator and verifier are also included in the NCVQ approved unit of qualification for Assessors. But this book is aimed primarily at Assessors, not the managers of Assessors, so I have excluded the coordinator and verifier roles summarised in the box on p 115.

I have also slightly re-organised the presentation of the Assessor roles from the official format and added my own standards 1, 2, and 4 which the NCVQ feel are self-evident.

So what makes a good Assessor?

The Riverside College of Health studies provides a wide range of nursing and health care courses leading to various professional, clinical and NVQ qualifications. Patrick Laryea is a principal lecturer and is responsible for the NVQ assessment process in the College. He was trained as an Assessor by the National Health Service and subsequently was interviewed and assessed himself to become an NCVQ appointed Assessor and internal verifier. Patrick feels several things are important in becoming a good Assessor:

> 'You need a sense of fairness and willingness to treat people as candidates not entities. You should not behave in a manner which may create anxiety in the individual you are assessing. You are not there to fail a person, but to help them realise their potential. You've got to encourage them.'

Patrick stresses the importance of teaching those planning to be Assessors the importance of listening, responding and questioning:

> 'An assessment environment is not cold: it has a dynamic and interactivity. The Assessor needs to appreciate this and use his or her skills. An Assessor gives information, guidance, is open, acts as a catalyst to point the candidate in the right direction. Therefore you need to be good at observation and direct the individual as to how they could do better. The role is much more than telling people whether they have passed or failed. It is important to give feedback, therefore there is an obvious link with teaching.'

Patrick believes that the role of assessor could be enhanced by more opportunities for reflection. Self-help peer groups of Assessors should meet regularly to learn more about their own sense of fairness and how they judge. Notes should be compared regularly and Assessors should feel encouraged to learn from the experience of their peers. Currently, the College holds three-monthly peer support meetings for

NVQ Assessors. These are always chaired and are recognised as an important part of the Assessor's own development.

Keith Walton, our experienced independent Assessor, comments:

> 'In assessing evidence, you've got to have people who know what they are doing . . . people who are able to balance between rigorous observation of standards and the reality of the situations the candidates are in. Candidates can never show enough evidence. The Assessor has to make a judgement as to when the assessment has to stop. In my experience, it can usually stop earlier than people think. Very importantly, assessment has to be holistic and positive. By that, I mean evidence must be seen as a whole and the Assessor must judge what the candidate can do, not look mainly for the gaps.'

Sue Edwards, our other independent Assessor, believes that

> 'if you know the performance criteria well enough, then not having done the specific job does not matter. The main skills are the ability to encourage and provide feedback; to recognise evidence that speaks for itself; to record accurately and allowing the candidate enough time to develop and compile evidence. You have to avoid becoming too much of a counsellor, yet you have to use your counselling skills to ask the right questions and probe for knowledge and understanding so that you can make good judgements. You must also like helping people to develop and have respect and commitment to candidates as adult learners.'

Kathleen Johnstone of North West Water points out that

> 'in larger organisations there are opportunities for candidates to work in groups and the Assessment Adviser and the Assessor should actively seek these out. The APL process is also an opportunity for the managers, Coaches and Mentors to develop themselves and adequate contact with the Assessor will help this process as well as benefiting the Assessors.'

The overlap between the role of the Qualifier Coach and the Mentor involved in the qualification process and the Assessment Adviser will now be obvious. Many of the skills for each of these roles will be similar but some skills will need to be applied differently.

Building rapport, as an Assessor must do with a candidate, may often happen over a shorter timescale than when acting as a Coach or Mentor. In some circumstances, it may be comparable to the relationship you had with your driving examiner! You were probably nervous enough anyway so remember that. It is essential to be friendly but purposeful. The Assessor needs to give encouragement and support to a reasonable extent but also to remain detached and objective.

The feedback following an assessment is also somewhat different from that following a coaching session. You need to give an easy to understand interpretation of your judgement. Identifying strengths and weaknesses and making suggestions for sensible plans for further training will be important. Clearly more sensitivity will be needed when you are telling unhappy candidates that they are not yet competent and have still more to do to prove their competence. They will need their confidence and motivation boosted to encourage them to continue.

Another important skill for the vocational qualification Assessor is the skilful administration of the assessment process itself. There are a number of different aspects to this broad skill:

- Thorough preparation. For example, if running an assessment session, are there suitable rooms, seating, work surfaces, space for invigilation, lighting, heating, ventilation, acoustics and freedom from unnecessary distractions?
- Accurate record-keeping is essential. Who was assessed, when and where, what methods were used, any unusual happenings (like fire alarms going off) which might have affected performance, what evidence was collected and what decision made?

The assessment session itself must be correctly handled and the following points should be followed:

- Provide proper introductions and explanations of the purpose and form of the assessment.
- Always give clear and concise instructions, standardised wherever possible; always stick to the precise wording of instructions; do not give candidates help or advice which will give them an advantage over other candidates who do not get the same information.
- Ensure at the end of an assessment session that candidates know what will happen next.
- Only release information to those who have a right to know – confidentiality of information is vital.

You must ensure common standards and delivery of assessment methods because it is an offence under the Race Relations and Equal

Opportunities Acts to use different methods with different groups.

Finally, you must ensure strict time-keeping both in the sense of only allowing the prescribed amount of time on a timed assessment and sticking to an assessment schedule. There is nothing worse than having candidates hanging around waiting for their turn.

Whether you are assessing performance in the general sense or specifically for a vocational qualification, there are a whole range of issues to be considered. The following checklist may help you concentrate on the essentials.

Checklist

1. Give plenty of notice, 1–2 weeks, of the time and place that the assessment will take place and make sure you arrive early to ensure that everything you need is available.
2. Check that the person you are assessing is ready and has prepared thoroughly; if they are not, rearrange the assessment to suit their needs.
3. Do your own preparation and homework thoroughly so that you know the areas you want to focus on and the questions you want to raise.
4. At the beginning of the assessment, clarify that the targets or criteria are understood by both of you.
5. If you are following a checklist approach, make sure that you don't miss key points but, if you are assessing from a range of evidence, balance the need for thoroughness with a realistic view of the time and economics involved; never skimp or rush.
6. Distinguish between progress, which should be encouraged, and achievement which means that targets and criteria have genuinely been met.
7. Be sensitive to age differences and the anxieties that people will experience during an assessment which is an important moment in their careers.
8. When giving feedback remember the three Cs: it should be clear, constructive and confidence-boosting.
9. Consult with other people involved in the process and ensure that the paperwork they require to monitor it is promptly and accurately completed.
10. Remember that, ultimately, the Assessor is interested only in the achievement of competent performance for the benefit of the organisation and the individual – be supportive.

CHAPTER 7
How Can I Listen and Observe Efficiently?

There is an old saying that God gave us two eyes, two ears but only one mouth so that we could look and listen four times as much as we speak. Certainly, I have come increasingly to realise that talking is not the main part of the communication process. But not everyone appreciates this. How often have you attended communication courses where the tutor spends most of the time explaining how you can structure your presentation or use visual aids but little, if any, on improving your listening skills?

More attention is sometimes paid to the ability of observing skills. If you have participated in games or exercises where several people are shown the same picture and asked to describe what they see, you will know that the result is often contradictory interpretations. All kinds of obstacles impair visual communication – and not just poor eyesight! People's explanations, assumptions, prejudices, wishes, all influence the messages they receive from observing and listening. Coaches, Mentors and Assessors rely heavily on these skills and need to be able to apply them effectively.

A Coach, for instance, operating in a hands-on role needs to listen to a learner's reply, not only for clarity but also for confidence in the learner's voice. This will confirm if they have really understood the Coach's instruction. Confidence and other emotions will most likely be expressed in the tone of the response rather than the words used. A Coach in a hands-off role has to rely very heavily on the skill of questioning to help the learner improve their performance, and has therefore to listen and interpret the response and at the same time decide very quickly on the next appropriate question to be effective. Pausing to reflect on the answer given is often a sensible technique. But having to ask for the answer to be repeated because of lazy listening will damage the Coach's credibility.

Mentors will often hold sessions in their own office. Failure to arrange for phone calls to be diverted can result in unnecessary interruptions to listening. For the Assessor who has to observe competent performance in the workplace and follow that up with questions, there is very little room for individual interpretation. If qualifications of competence are to have credibility and validity, it is essential that any number of Assessors observing the same demonstration of performance and listening to the same answers would make the same judgement as to the competence of the candidate.

It isn't simple

The first rule of observation therefore must be 'it isn't as simple as you might think'. The second rule should be 'Be sure you would recognise competence when you see it'. If in any doubt, check thoroughly before you begin. For the Assessor, the detailed performance criteria provide an essential reference point. But it is useful to confirm with other Assessors and experts on a regular basis to make sure that you still know what you are looking for.

Observing is not necessarily a step-by-step, easy to follow process but is often continuous with lots of things happening at once. Take the example (discussed in more detail in Chapter 4) of the Coach during a session with the horserider preparing for a competition. Just imagine what that Coach had to observe while the rider was practising even a simple movement:

- what aids did the rider use?
- how did the horse respond?
- what went well and why?
- what went wrong and why?
- how could it have been improved?
- was the pace right?
- was the rider's position right?
- did the horse keep a correct outline?
- did the horse resist and why?
- what was the general overall impression?

Take another example of an Assessor observing a salesperson in a sales interview:

- how did they greet the customer?
- what was the initial reaction?
- what questions were asked?
- how well did the salesperson listen?
- which products were presented in which order?
- to what extent was the customer involved?
- how were objections handled?
- how were the sales aids used?
- did the salesperson handle technical questions knowledgeably?
- how did the salesperson gain commitment or take an order?
- what was missing?
- how did the buyer react throughout the interview?
- which aspects of the interview went well?
- what could have been done better?

These and many other observations have to be noted as they occur. Learning to concentrate and interpret what you see is really hard work. Note-taking is essential; relying on memory means that important points are sometimes missed. Taking notes is not easy for some people but, with practice, the skill can be acquired. Noting key words or phrases is one technique; mind maps referred to in Chapter 1 is another. Having a sensible sized pad and a pen available is an obvious tip that is sometimes forgotten. Some assessment processes require you to follow a checklist approach but noting down additional points will always be helpful.

These examples also illustrate another difficulty associated with observing. Had the Coach or Assessor become actively involved with either of the instances described, it may have reduced the validity of the observations and subsequent feedback or assessment. Unobtrusive observation and restraining the impulse to intervene is therefore an important skill to develop.

The importance of body language

Imagine a situation where you, as a Mentor, choose to hold a session with two protégés at the same time. This could be at the end of an assignment or prior to an assessment. One protégé sits with arms folded, feet tapping and replies in a terse but perfectly accurate way.

The other protégé is sitting forward comfortably, arms on the table, looking you straight in the eyes and answering calmly but in an equally accurate way. If you are only listening to the verbal answers you will receive one set of messages, but by observing consciously at the same time, you will also receive what are described as non-verbal messages. These messages can be equally important.

Choosing which are the most important messages can sometimes pose a dilemma, particularly for an Assessor. If you are assessing objectively, you should perhaps not pay too much attention to body language and concentrate on what is actually said and what you actually see being done. Animated body language during an assessment could simply arise from nerves or habit. But for the Mentor or Coach the non-verbal signs may be important clues to unspoken development needs.

To help resolve these dilemmas, it is important to appreciate the basics of non-verbal communication, or body language as it is termed. Facial expressions, gestures, posture, eye signals, body movements, all transmit a message. Body language, it is claimed, can be a window to our thoughts, indeed it often speaks louder than words – we may say one thing, while our bodies say another. Some of the key non-verbal signs are:

- Empathy can be signalled by smiles, open and positive gestures, standing or sitting close, eye contact or nodding and tilting the head.
- A defensive or distrusting attitude can be signalled if someone sits with their crossed leg towards you while a willingness to trust can be signalled if the crossed leg is away from you.
- Anger or aggression can be signalled by a rigid or tense body posture, staring eyes, clenched fists or clasped hands, tightly folded arms, foot tapping and finger pointing.
- Nervousness can be signalled by downcast eyes, hand over the mouth or frequently touching the face, shifting weight or fidgeting.
- Boredom can be signalled by picking imaginary fluff from sleeves, pulling at ear, stifled yawning or gazing around the room.

A useful book which will give you more information on this important skill is *Body Language* by Alan Pease. One word of caution: you will note that I have said only that these signals can *indicate* the different emotions. One gesture on its own almost certainly won't be enough to draw a conclusion. It is a continuance or combination of non-verbal signals that you need to learn to interpret. Not only must we recognise all these gestures in others, but we must guard against our own body language as it may be interpreted by others in the same way!

It is also important to remember that, although people in the same culture or from the same country send and receive similar non-verbal signals, people from other cultures or countries may interpret them differently. For example, in Britain people signal numbers with their fingers by using the index finger as number one. However, in Germany, if you put up your index finger for a beer in a bar, you're likely to be served two – they use the thumb to signify number one. Another example of cultural differences is that an OK signal formed by creating an O with your finger and thumb means OK to the English or Americans but to the French it means zero or no good at all! As an example of cultural differences, the eye contact rules used by Africans for showing interest and paying attention are opposite to those of Europeans who often misinterpret this different behaviour as rudeness or sullenness. Styles of spoken communication can also differ markedly. Certain Asian groups tend to give very detailed responses which are sometimes considered by non-Asians to be irritatingly long-winded.

Awareness of body space

There is another aspect of body language which should be considered within our context. This is the need to be sensitive to the area or space that a person claims as their own, as if it were an extension of their body. People tend to regard their office, desk, chair and the space surrounding any of their possessions as 'their territory'. To make yourself at home by immediately sitting down and placing your belongings on their desk may well be offensive and invasive to that person.

There are also what are termed 'personal zones'. These are usually determined by culture and therefore can differ. As a rule, what is termed the 'intimate zone' is that area very jealously guarded by us all. Move within 6–18 inches of somebody and they may well immediately feel uncomfortable and even threatened, unless of course you have an intimate personal relationship! Research has shown that people from the country need greater space than those from towns and cities. Another example is entering a crowded lift. You will notice that often, if it is very crowded, people tend to look up at the floor level indicator light, rather than at each other, mainly because they feel too close together. Research suggests that these behaviours relate to the very strong impulses that body space causes.

If you want people to feel at ease in your presence, keep to the distance within which people feel most comfortable. An arm's length is a good guide. It is important also to think carefully about the positioning of desks, tables and seating arrangements for a mentoring or coaching session. A competitive or defensive position may be created when a desk or table forms a barrier between two people sitting directly opposite each other. They are forced quite literally to take sides. This does nothing to enhance openness or cooperation, trust and harmony. To avoid this, salespeople are often encouraged to move round to the customer's side of the desk when demonstrating or illustrating a particular point. This is done to create a feeling of togetherness as opposed to a 'you-and-us' relationship. It also allows the customer to avoid the salesperson's face which means that, if necessary, they can look away with ease. This sales technique has to be handled with care to avoid the negative reaction of invading personal space.

Trust and distrust

Eyes often give the most accurate and revealing signals of all. The expression 'we see eye to eye' indicates that agreement can be signalled by eye contact. Acceptable eye contact is usually in the area of 60–70 per cent during the course of a conversation. If the other person either hardly looks at you or stares at you all the time, there is a tendency to immediately regard them with distrust and suspicion.

It is claimed that body language can be the most important part of any message. Some estimate that it accounts for at least 55 per cent. When the words spoken conflict with the body language, the receiver tends to believe the non-verbal message. For example, you are busy but a colleague asks you for a few minutes of your time. You easily agree: 'No problem, I've always got time for you.' Soon however you are looking at your watch and shifting in your seat. All the signals suggest you haven't got the time despite what you said. If your colleague is alert and sensitive to these gestures, they will curtail the conversation and leave rather than risk upsetting your relationship. Similarly, how many times have you seen a child look at the floor and deny that they've 'done wrong'? You are strongly inclined to believe the stance and gestures, not the verbal denial.

Myths and prejudices

It is important also to guard against your own prejudices and avoid stereotyping people when interpreting messages. Some people for instance believe that people with public school accents or who wear glasses are automatically more clever than other people. Another common myth or fallacy is that older people find it harder to learn new things than younger people.

When you stop to think about these issues it soon becomes clear that they are unlikely to be true. But there is a real danger of allowing first impressions to affect your judgement. In an assessment situation, this can be particularly dangerous as you need to listen and observe throughout the session to make an objective judgement. Of course candidates can try to mislead you. Someone who answers in a confident manner or appears to agree with everything you say may create a more positive attitude than their level of performance deserves. There is a technical term called the 'halo effect' which also should be understood. This warns of the danger of allowing one impression or piece of evidence to outweigh all the other evidence. Apparently we are all open to this type of misjudgement, particularly where one strong negative impression blinds us to an accurate and objective interpretation.

Active listening

I have concentrated so far mainly on observation skills but many of these issues also relate to listening. So let's discuss listening in more detail. It is useful to recognise that there are different levels of listening. 'Peripheral' listening is done at a subconscious level and can occur in formal or informal situations. For example, you may be in a busy restaurant talking with people at your table but also picking up snippets of conversation from another table. 'Apparent' listening is what we all do most of the time. We look as if we are listening but in fact we are not really concentrating. 'Active' or effective listening is often what we should be doing. This involves really concentrating on the message being transmitted by trying to understand not only what is being said but how and why it is being said.

It is the ability to listen actively that separates the good communicators from the poor. Like any skills, effective listening requires self-discipline and practice and it is certainly hard work. It is estimated that most people talk at a rate of 125 words per minute but that they can think at up to four times that speed. This means that as a listener you have a spare mental capacity which, if you do not discipline yourself, results in mind wandering and lack of concentration. We have all experienced a tuning in and out of conversations or discussions and then having to ask for something to be repeated because we have missed a key point of the message.

Success as a Coach, Mentor or Assessor depends on the ability to concentrate efficiently on what is being said, often for long periods. You may well make a learner, protégé or candidate feel unimportant or insignificant if they sense their ideas and feelings are not being paid close attention. The relationship then undoubtedly will suffer. The temptation to only half listen is of course very real. Having asked a question, if you get an early indication that the answer is going to be correct, or what you were expecting, there is an inclination to switch off before the end of the response. By doing so you risk missing some enlightening, new information or indeed additional information which shows that your initial assumptions were incorrect. Similarly, you may be so preoccupied formulating your next question that you miss at least part of the response to your current question.

So what does active listening involve? What do we mean by active listening? The process is as follows: having received a response there is *interpretation* of what was heard, leading to *understanding*. Then comes *evaluation*, or weighing the information, comparing it with existing knowledge and deciding what to do with it. Based on your understanding and evaluation, you *react* by *planning* your reply and then you *respond*. Understanding this process will help you adopt a disciplined approach to active listening.

What cannot be ignored in this process is of course the way in which a response is delivered. It is estimated that tone counts for as much as one-third of a message. An active listener must be alert to any emphasis on certain words, also to fluency, or lack of fluency, as well as by emotional language. In the same way, they must listen for the meaning behind the words. If a learner says 'the main reason is . . .', this could imply there are other considerations which may need exploring. Only by active listening will what is *not* said be identified.

Active listening requires planning and practice. We have to work at it and like all other skills, we need to be interested and motivated enough to want real results from our efforts. So, how do you go about putting all this into practice? Let me suggest a three-stage process for efficient listening.

Stage one

Carefully select the location (whenever possible):

- choose a quiet room or area free from the distraction of other people and noise;
- arrange seating to avoid any physical barriers such as a desk, but don't sit too close;
- set aside any other work you are doing;
- arrange for telephone calls to be diverted;
- remove or ignore any other distractions;
- shut the door, if possible.

Stage two

Create the right atmosphere:

- look interested and maintain eye contact without staring;
- be patient – allow the person time to say all they want to say (within reason);
- always use their first name;
- maintain a relaxed posture;
- be encouraging by leaning forward, nodding, putting your head to one side, smiling whenever appropriate.

Stage three

Practise helpful listening behaviour:

- make listening noises: eg 'Mmmm', 'Yes', 'I see';
- pause before responding to indicate that you are digesting what has been said;
- keep an open mind – do not pre-judge people, jump to conclusions or interrupt;
- suspend prejudice; don't allow the fact you disagreed make you turn a deaf ear to what is being said;
- concentrate on what matters by trying to get at the core of the response;
- be sensitive to mood, facial expressions and body movements to understand the full meaning of what is being said;
- plan to make a report to someone else following the meeting and imagine they are the sort of person who likes to know all the details of what you have heard;
- seek more information by repeating or paraphrasing;
- summarise to check your understanding.

Finally, make a habit of taking notes. As we have seen, listening only occupies something like one-third of our available mental capacity. The remaining two-thirds of the mind will wander if not otherwise used. But, more important, note-taking gives you a record of what you are hearing and helps to emphasise the importance you are placing on what is being said to you. Many of these helpful behaviours we have listed will be made easier by good and accurate note-taking, but it helps if you explain to the other person why you are taking notes.

Whether you are a Coach, Mentor or Assessor, effective observing and listening is key to all three roles. The Coach and Mentor will want to encourage responses that guide the learner or protégé to a solution. By definition, an Assessor is checking competence and confidence and will be looking and listening for evidence of knowledge and skill in more absolute terms. In either case, the ability to observe and listen effectively is crucial to the future development of the individuals. (For more on this subject, the book *Ways of Seeing* by John Berger is a useful source of reference.) The following checklist should prove a useful guide to improving the way you use your eyes and ears.

Checklist

1. Non-verbal signals are important and you should learn to recognise them.
2. Beware of cultural differences in communication habits.
3. Recognise that your own emotions affect the signals you send.
4. Don't let your own prejudices get in the way.
5. Concentrate and pay attention to details.
6. Take accurate notes to avoid misunderstanding.
7. How people say things is often as important as what they say.
8. If you want to learn you must be prepared to listen and show you are listening actively.
9. Establish the performance criteria before you begin to assess the messages you receive.
10. Plan in advance to avoid distractions.

CHAPTER 8

How Can I Ask the Right Question?

One of the oldest jokes I can remember is the story of the little boy standing outside the door of a house. A door-to-door salesman approaches him and asks 'Son, is your mother at home?' 'Yes,' replies the little boy. The salesman knocks on the door but receives no reply. After several minutes of knocking with no response he turns angrily to the boy and says, 'Hey, I thought you said your mother was at home.' 'She is,' replies the boy, 'but I don't live here!'

The moral of that story is that if you don't ask the right question you probably won't get the right answer. The combination of asking the right question because you know the subject matter well and asking the right question in the most appropriate way lies at the heart of skilled coaching, mentoring and assessing.

The skill and art of questioning is a well researched and documented subject, a useful reference is *How to Communicate* by G. Wells. Managers often receive detailed training on interviewing, appraising and counselling skills. Lawyers too have to develop the ability to cross-examine.

Coaches and Mentors need to learn the basics but should bear in mind that their primary role is to encourage and develop. This cannot be achieved if undue pressure is created by inept questioning. A meaningful coaching and/or mentoring session depends on using questions which provoke a response that enhances learning. It is important to build a relationship which is open and honest so that the learner or protégé can accept the sometimes painful process of being stretched by difficult questions. Asking embarrassing questions is likely to lead to defensive, negative responses and a deterioration of the relationship.

An Assessor, however, is primarily interested in questioning to establish facts and judge levels of competence against specific criteria. At the same time, Assessors have a responsibility to maintain rapport with the candidate so that a fair and just assessment is achieved. Assessing is not about putting people on the spot by loaded or trick questions but using specific types of questions to generate an appropriate response. Let us look at various questioning techniques.

Understanding the basics

Among the basic theoretical concepts of questioning is the importance of recognising that there are two main types of question, open and closed. A closed question is one that may be answered by a simple 'yes' or 'no' and usually begins with 'do you', 'are you', 'have you' and so on. On the other hand, open questions are aimed at provoking an extended response and might start with 'what', 'where', 'which', 'why', 'how' or 'when'.

Closed questions are appropriate:

- where a straightforward 'yes' or 'no' is enough;
- to verify information;
- to confirm understanding of facts;
- to confirm agreement or commitment;
- to get a decision when there are only two alternatives.

The repeated use of closed questions needs to be avoided because they can become very wearing on the respondent and can quickly turn into an interrogation.

A more difficult skill to develop is to be able to use open questions which enable the questioner to:

- establish rapport and put the other person at ease;
- encourage uninhibited feedback;
- help to explore opinions in more detail;
- create involvement and commitment;
- check out understanding more comprehensively.

For example, if you wanted to ask a candidate their opinion on, say, the merits of the local football team, you wouldn't say 'Do you agree that the local team is a good one?' This invites a simple yes or no response. If you had phrased the question 'What do you think are the good points about the local team?', you would instead invite a response that required the candidate to express an opinion. And if there were no good points, you have the opportunity to follow up with 'Well can you describe their weak points?'

Another example indicates the care Coaches and Mentors in particular need to exercise in selecting the best type of open question. If you want to encourage learners or protégés to develop their performance, you have also to help develop self-awareness, a sense of responsibility for future action and a commitment to persevere with the action. You will find that open questions like 'what happened?' and 'why did that happen?' tend to produce descriptive and potentially somewhat defensive responses, whereas questions like 'how did it feel when you were doing that?' or 'what do you imagine it would look like if you did it differently?' or 'what can you do to lift the performance still further?' will encourage responses that focus on positive ideas for future action. I would term these as 'awareness raising' questions. You can classify questions in other ways:

Reflective Questions
This type of question is a useful means of clarification. By taking what has been said and rephrasing and reflecting it back you test your own understanding and possibly encourage the other person to talk more. You can use questions like 'So what you mean is . . ., am I correct?' This gives the opportunity for the respondent to give additional information or to think of new ways of making their views clearer.

Justifying Questions
These questions provide an opportunity for further explanation of reasons, attitudes or feelings. Examples are 'What makes you . . .?', 'How do you explain . . .?' This type of question can provide very useful responses but can also be rather confrontational especially if delivered in a challenging tone or manner. Better sometimes to phrase them 'You say this but are you sure?', or 'Could you help me to understand your explanation by putting it another way?'

Hypothetical Questions
These are questions that pose a situation or a suggestion: 'what if . . .?', 'how about . . .?'. These can be useful if you want to introduce a new idea or concept, lead towards agreement, challenge a response without causing offence or defensiveness or check that you fully understand the implications of an earlier answer. Hypothetical questions can be very powerful and stretching in coaching, mentoring and assessing situations. But they should only be asked when it is reasonable

to expect the other person to have sufficient knowledge or understanding of the situation you are asking them to speculate about.

Probing Questions
These are often supplementary questions where the full information required has not been given as part of the initial response. The reason it has not been offered may be because the initial question was inappropriate or unclear. Alternatively the respondent may be deliberately not replying fully. Probing questions are among the most difficult to ask and may of course involve asking a mix of open, closed, reflective, justifying and hypothetical questions. Two basic probing techniques are *funnelling*, where you start with large, broad questions and gradually narrow the focus down to the specific information you are seeking, and *drilling*, where you decide in advance the question areas you want to pursue and dig deeper and deeper until you strike the response you have been looking for.

A disciplined approach

Once a question has been asked another skill - listening - comes into play. You need to develop the ability to stay silent. Having asked a question, it is important that you remain quiet to give time for the other person to reflect and respond at their own pace. Many of us are frightened of silence; we have an urge to say something, particularly if an immediate response is not forthcoming. Try not to do this because it can be a real hindrance in any coaching, mentoring or assessing situation where you are constantly aiming to encourage the other person to think for themselves to improve or demonstrate their competence. However, if your disciplined silence does not have the desired effect, you can either ask a direct 'closed' supplementary question or rephrase the question altogether. The important point is to get your timing right and, of course, avoiding the temptation to butt in and answer the question yourself! I think it is useful to use a model to illustrate the questioning structure (see Figure 8.1).

A question of style

It is important that you develop your own natural style of questioning. The most structured open question in the world will not produce the

FIG. 8.1 QUESTIONING MODEL

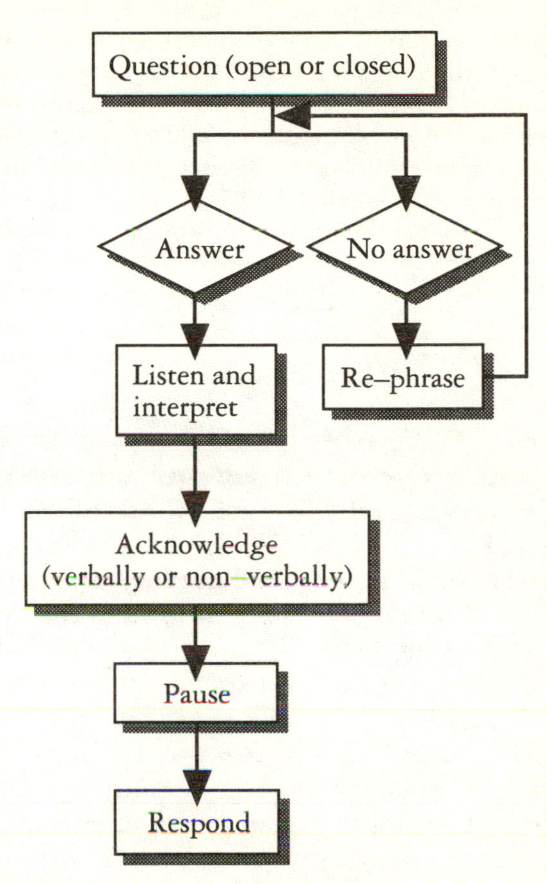

right response if it is delivered in an aggressive, condescending, or over-challenging manner. If, for example, you observe a silly mistake being made there may be a temptation to blurt out 'For Heaven's sake! Why on earth are you doing it that way?' The result may be that the mistake stops but it is also very likely that the response you get will be defensive and aggrieved. You may have caused demotivation as well. An alternative intervention might have been, 'Well, that doesn't seem to be working very well does it? Can you think of a different way of doing it?' This is much more controlled – and is not always easy to think of in the heat of the moment. The response it is likely to get, however, is much more positive. The action will have stopped. Measured criticism has been made and less defensiveness caused. And the person involved has been encouraged to think for themselves of an alternative, and better, way of completing the task. This process is obviously more time-consuming than a simple 'look, let me show you' intervention but the outcome is worth it. Again the tone you use to ask this type of question is important. You have to avoid the condescending, patronising approach as this will negate the effort you have made.

Getting the right response to your questioning is such an important skill that I have treated it in isolation. The following checklist of Dos and Don'ts will help you get the answer you want.

Checklist

Positive response

1. Always prepare questions in advance; it always produces benefits and is the first golden rule of effective questioning.
2. Work hard to build rapport and put the other person at ease and always clearly state the aim of the questioning at the start.
3. Try to ask clear, concise and specific questions.
4. Always acknowledge answers positively and in an encouraging tone.
5. Do consider answers before responding, often deliberately pausing to create the right effect.
6. Do use silence when appropriate (it may intimidate so be careful, but it can provide additional sensitive information as respondents may feel the need to keep talking).
7. Do probe for extra information if you suspect more is available.
8. Always check your understanding by summarising and using reflective questions.

Negative response

1. Don't ask long-winded questions, they will probably be misunderstood.
2. Don't ask multiple questions; people inevitably choose the easiest answers first and avoid the difficult one you really wanted to know the answer to.
3. Don't ask leading or loaded questions; they usually only demonstrate what *you* know rather than what the respondent really knows or thinks.
4. Don't ask trick questions unless you can explain the purpose because they cause resentment and demotivation.
5. Don't use complex inappropriate language; you simply want to be understood.
6. Don't assume the answer or jump to the conclusion that what you hear first is the complete answer.
7. Don't be side-tracked by answers that are interesting but not relevant to the performance standard.

CHAPTER 9
How Can I Set Goals to Develop Competence?

It is almost impossible to overestimate the importance of setting goals in the context of developing competence. As we examine the issues in more detail, it will also become obvious what a key role questioning skills play in goal setting.

In a perfectly logical world people would always sit down and draw up a plan to achieve their most important goals. In reality, of course, many people have only very dreamy or wishful ideas of what their major goals in life are. 'I want to be a millionaire' or 'I want to be a filmstar' may well be how a young school-leaver would state their goal. But, as they soon realise, they cannot fly to their goals in one go but must slowly and painstakingly build a ladder, rung by rung, even to begin to approach them.

From the example in Chapter 4 of David Hemery's methodical approach to winning his Olympic gold medal it becomes clear that there are different types of goals. The key to understanding goal setting is to realise that, in order to achieve the most important ones, it is necessary to set many smaller goals within goals, which some people prefer to call performance targets. The smaller the goal, the shorter its timescale should be. It is easier then to keep it in sharp focus and avoid being knocked off course by unforeseen events.

Career goals also come in different sizes. Within an overall career plan, which may spiral up into being managing director or earning a six-figure salary, there will be yearly, monthly, weekly and even daily goals. It is this development of career goals that, to different degrees, the Coach, Mentor and Assessor are concerned with. It may well be that the Mentor helps focus on longer-term objectives while the

Coach takes on the responsibility of helping to achieve shorter-term plans. The Assessor's role in this context might be described as evaluating to what extent performance goals have been fulfilled. Whatever the individual roles, everyone needs to recognise the value of being able to set goals properly. And this process of setting goals can be divided into the four stages of the typical problem solving model we have used in other chapters, namely analysing the situation, planning solutions, implementing the plan and evaluating the results.

Analysing the situation

Before any realistic goals can be set, a starting point must be established. An analysis of where the learner, protégé or candidate is, is a prerequisite to deciding where they should go. At as early a stage as possible it may be helpful if broad, long-term goals can be identified. For example, a Mentor might discover that a young sales trainee has ambitions of being a senior manager within 10 years. Beyond that the goal is vague and uncertain. Although 10 years is a distant ambition rather than a tangible goal, it provides both a focus and a direction for the goal setting process.

The Mentor's task is to get trainees to recognise for themselves the various stages that might be required. Using skilful questioning the trainee could probably be helped to recognise a progression from field sales, to product management, to budget and financial management and then to senior management. Careful probing by the Mentor could also enable the trainee to identify the gaps that exist in their experience and thus perhaps to see the benefit of gaining a professional qualification. The first step – or mini-goal – might then be to become accepted on a study course. The next performance target might be to complete the course successfully.

The major benefit of the Mentor using skilful questioning rather than prescribing a solution is that the trainee, having worked out the answers, will be more likely to 'own' the solution. Without ownership and commitment the chances of achieving the goal are much slimmer.

Once an ultimate goal and a series of performance targets have been identified the next step in analysing the situation is to appraise honestly the learner's strengths and weaknesses. It is vital to get as complete a picture as possible of the learner's abilities and potential before attempting to finalise goals. It may be tempting for a Mentor who has discovered what various protégés' long-term career goals are then to prescribe several brilliant plans, carefully contrived to take them there step by step via monthly and weekly targets. All the protégés then have to do is follow the Mentor's plan. It's a logical process which can't fail to yield the desired results – but are they really capable? Do they yet have the inter-personal skills needed to manage 20 staff? Do they all have the self-confidence to battle for budgets? From the Mentor's position as a senior manager, it is sometimes difficult to recognise a protégé's limitations. Overoptimism can be very counter-productive at this point. Realism may take longer but it is more certain.

The process of assessment should be undertaken by the learners themselves. Coaches, Mentors and Assessment Advisers must be involved but it is the learner who has to decide where they are currently in performance terms. In Chapter 1, 'How Do Adults Learn?', I suggested how a self-assessment process might work and, of course, it applies to this situation also.

Performance goals should, as far as possible, represent a clear route which stretches from the current situation to the ultimate goal. The current situation can be defined as the present moment, by which I mean the precise moment when the session of coaching, mentoring or assessment is actually occurring. Every one of these sessions should start by agreeing the goals for that session that day. This disciplined approach will pay dividends. It will focus regularly on achievement; and if the goal for the session is not achieved, you can spend time analysing the reasons why. Again, the use of skilful questioning to get the learner to identify any faults and the most appropriate solutions will reinforce the sense of ownership and commitment to the development programme.

Planning solutions

Choosing the best option to achieve a goal is an important step towards achieving it. Different people have very different ways of approaching tasks. But even the supreme activist should have some plan before diving in. Many people would rather do something than think carefully about what they're doing. There's nothing wrong with itching to get started but it can be counter-productive to head off at full speed in altogether the wrong direction. Action itself is often easy but action that takes you quickly and efficiently to where you want to be is more likely if it is properly planned.

Sometimes a goal requires action which seems so obvious it hardly seems worth planning. For example, if the goal is to pass the driving test in three months, the action plan might appear to be to get some driving lessons as soon as possible. But what about some additional (and more inexpensive) practice sessions with a friend or relative? What about obtaining a provisional licence and making the appointment for the test? Even simple goals require proper planning. They also require a thorough review of all the options available. While the shortest distance between two points mathematically is a straight line, life is rarely that simple and there are a wide range of options available.

If a structure of planning forms on the lines suggested in this book is not available, an alternative is to start by writing down two lists. The first should include everything you can think of that you believe must be done if the goal is to be hit. The second should be a list of performances you do *not* want to see; things that would have a negative effect on your goal. For example, if your goal is to increase sales by x per cent in a year you might include on your first list: send a Christmas card to all existing clients; train the sales force to be more friendly on the telephone; commission a study on the efficiency of different advertising media, etc. On the second list you might have: shoddy appearance at client meetings; lack of up to date market research; badly prepared presentations and so on.

By the time you've finished, what you should have in front of you is a list of outcomes that have to be achieved before you can realistically expect your goals to be hit. In other words, you have identified the goal elements: the performances and achievements that go to make up the goal itself. You will also most probably have crossed out some ideas or options that on reflection you did not want to follow. Do not be afraid to consider a whole range of possibilities. Even the most way-out ideas sometimes help to focus your mind on the most appropriate option to choose eventually.

Smart goals

All goals should satisfy certain basic criteria which can be neatly summed up by using the same acronym that ICI Pharmaceuticals used in their performance review process, SMART:

- Stretching
- Measurable
- Achievable

- Relevant
- Time-framed

Stretching
For someone who wants to improve their performance it is not particularly helpful to set a goal that is well within their current capabilities. Motivation and achievement are more likely if the goal set stretches the performer some way beyond their present performance level.

Measurable
'If you can't measure it you can't manage it' is a quite well-known phrase. If you cannot define or measure a goal accurately, how can you know if it has been achieved? Agreeing the method of measurement at the beginning is vital too. Is it to be additional sales or output or faster delivery or all three? And precisely how much more or how much faster? Vagueness will result in conflicts and disappointments if the goal is not achieved. But a precise target to aim at is very motivating.

Achievable
A performer has to believe that a goal is reasonably within their scope. Setting a young recruit the goal of writing a report for the board on the subject of the latest technology or the company's prospects over the next five years is likely to be so far beyond the recruit's capability that nothing will be achieved except frustration and demotivation. Setting them the goal of researching the literature to help the manager write the report is more likely to be seen as achievable.

Overoptimistic goal setting can be more dangerous than setting goals that do not stretch a performer. 'Trebling sales for the next period' may sound fine but how realistic is it? Are the customers there? Is the product available and at the right price? These are just a few of the questions that need to be answered. The practicalities, based on previous experience, must always be rigorously analysed to ensure that goals are realistic.

Relevant
Relevance is a key aspect of motivating people to achieve goals. Asking people to perform irrelevant tasks is the quickest way to ensure that they 'switch off'. All performance goals need to be accepted by a performer as relevant to their current goals, ambitions or career plans. It is important too that an individual's goals are relevant to the organisational goals and business objectives. If senior managers do not share an individual's goals they are unlikely to be supportive in

achieving them. Sometimes an individual's personal goals may not be in harmony with the organisation they are working for and this is obviously a potential source of frustration and demotivation. Ultimately, only by talking honestly to a Mentor or some other appropriate adviser will the issues be clarified. But pretending that this clash of objectives does not exist will help no one.

Time-framed
Improving performance by a measurable amount is one dimension of a good goal. But in what time-frame? Will it be a week, month or year? Without a realistic, achievable but stretching time-frame that goal of measured improvements may never be reached. Gaining commitment to a definite time to start and to complete a task is the best way to ensure that the will to achieve it really exists.

Implementation

A well-structured plan that is written down and 'signed-off' by everyone involved should make implementation appear straightforward. But, as everyone knows when they make a New Year's resolution, it is one thing to set a task, another actually to do it!

The Coach, Mentor and Assessor will need to recognise their responsibility for maintaining the motivation of their performers. They need to provide support, encouragement and help in overcoming obstacles that inevitably occur. Regular meetings will be needed to monitor progress and help realign or modify the approach the performer is taking. The ultimate responsibility lies with the performer but as the case studies in other chapters have shown the level of support provided is absolutely crucial during an implementation phase.

Evaluating results

If the goal has satisfied the SMART criteria it will be measurable. This means that there will be no ambiguity as to whether it has been achieved or not. However, because the goal is also designed to be stretching it may not always be reached. It may therefore sometimes be a mistake for a Coach or Mentor to evaluate success merely by whether or not it has been achieved in total. We have all probably been advised when we were younger to 'aim high' by a parent or a tutor. This does not mean they necessarily expect us to come top of the class simply by aiming for it. But they believed that by aiming for the top we have a greater chance of, say, coming in the top 10 than if we started out with more modest targets. Equally, just because a goal has not been fully attained, it does not mean that nothing of value has been gained.

This approach may be realistic and pragmatic for the Coach and Mentor but is it really an option for the Assessor? The Coach and Mentor are primarily concerned in helping to develop competence and if it takes longer to achieve than planned then their role can continue. An Assessor's primary role, however, is to judge whether criteria have or have not been met at that moment in time. Evaluation is usually a clean-cut issue although there will always be marginal cases. An Assessor, of course, must be able and willing to recognise and value progress towards achievement of a goal. But progress towards a goal is not the same as achieving it. An Assessor has a fine balancing act to perform between objective judgement and the need to continue to motivate.

SMART goals and a planned approach are the key to effective goal setting. Using SMART as a checklist is the most helpful tip I can give. It is easy to remember and easy to apply.

Checklist

1. **What is another name for goals?**
2. **What are the four stages of the problem-solving model?**
3. **What does the acronym SMART stand for?**
4. **Think of a personal goal of your own. Are the SMART criteria satisfied?**

CHAPTER 10

How Can I Give Feedback Which Builds Confidence and Success?

One interesting definition of human communication is 'the passing and receiving of messages between two or more people in order that both sender and receiver may act appropriately on their interpretation of the messages they receive'. The beauty of this definition is that it stresses that communication is a two-way process that leads to appropriate action. But it also emphasises the equal importance of responding to sending and that feedback is fundamental to effective communication. In the context of developing competence, it is not an exaggeration to describe feedback as 'the fuel that drives improved performance'.

Coaches, Mentors and Assessors will often find themselves in feedback situations. Inexperienced learners want to ask 'How well am I doing?' Candidates are always interested to know 'Have I proved my competence?' An experienced learner attempting to improve their performance still further might say 'If I do it this way I think it will be better; what do you think?' A protégé may say to a Mentor 'I have the chance to apply for this new job, do you think I should do it?' Deciding on the appropriate feedback needs careful thought.

Sensitivity and stress

Many young people are shy and feel awkward and embarrassed in new situations where they have to perform alongside other experienced staff. More experienced people on a learning programme can also feel inhibited and unable to relax in the same way that they can in their usual work role. Helping people whose self-image may not be too high by guiding them towards early successes, encouraging positive behaviour and rewarding efforts contributes towards the development of a positive 'I *can* do it' attitude.

Coaches, Mentors and Assessors need to be sensitive to the mental state of the people they are working with. And of course they must be sensitive also to their own mental state because feedback is a two-way process. In stressful situations people react differently and not always in the most appropriate manner. It would be a mistake to underestimate how stressful some will find both a coaching and mentoring session and of course an assessment coming at the end of a period of learning will often cause great anxiety. Transactional Analysis (TA) is one approach to understanding the basics of the differing mental states people have in relationships. A transaction can be defined as a signal or stimulus from one person to another, and the signal or response sent back in reply. One signal and its reply is followed by another so feedback becomes a series of transactions.

Transactional Analysis suggests that there are three predominant states and that we all respond in any one of these, depending on our mood and the pressure of the situation. The sensitivity lies in recognising, selecting or managing our own behaviour to respond in the most appropriate state to match both the situation and the mental state of other people involved. Briefly, the description of these ego states is:

- Parent state - which consists of our beliefs, values, standards and morals. We calculate and judge in this state. We can also adopt either a critical or caring outlook to the other person.
- Adult state - which consists of our rational, unemotional and analytical outlook. We are happy in this state to consider reality, facts and figures, we readily engage in problem solving and discuss calmly the implications of our decisions.
- Child state - which consists of spontaneous, fun-loving and natural reactions to events. We are curious, creative and jokey in this state. On the other hand we may act in an emotionally, irrationally petulant and sulky way just like spoilt children who can't get their own way.

The states could be summarised as parent (beliefs), adult (thinking) and child (feeling). People continuously swap and change between the three. Understanding the basics of TA and the ego states can help us to be aware of our mental state before or during a situation. This helps us respond accordingly to avoid clashes which occur when ego states become crossed rather than complementing or parallel. The aim is often to get both people operating in their adult ego state, so that they can review facts, examine solutions and implications without crossed transactions creating too many obstacles of beliefs and prejudices or feelings and emotions. Reading the book *How to Develop a Positive Attitude* by Elwood N. Chapman would help Coaches, Mentors and Assessors to understand these issues more fully.

Maintaining progress

During a development process, one of the best ways to build confidence is regularly to monitor progress. 'How am I doing?' is a reasonable question the learner will want to ask. For development to occur, the learner often needs to be reassured that they are beginning to perform closer to the standard or goal agreed earlier. Regular reviews act as a vehicle to reinforce effective performance, highlight areas for improvement and recognise developing strengths and potential weaknesses. Obstacles or barriers to performance can be discussed and joint actions planned, to overcome them or, if necessary, to modify the programme.

Whenever a review takes place it should start by revisiting the goals. If a qualification is the goal, how is the learner progressing against the syllabus or development plan? What do results from tutors' reports indicate? If the acquisition of new knowledge or skills is the goal, how has the learner performed in post-learning tests or in applying the information gained? A consistent, well-organised and systematic approach by the Coach, Mentor or Assessor is one of the surest ways to build confidence in their learner, protégé or candidate.

Retaining control over situations or events is crucial for a development plan to be successful and some things are outside the learner's control. For example, a Mentor responsible for an individual's introduction to the organisation may have to intervene to resolve the reassignment of their work priorities by the individual's manager, to allow completion of the development plan.

To maintain progress and help encourage a positive attitude, review sessions should get the learner to highlight achievements and reflect on difficulties that have been overcome. Comparing progress to the original plan and recognising the passing of milestones helps to show accomplishment by the learner. This also provides an excellent opportunity to reward and celebrate successes with the learner, who may be too modest to acknowledge these events.

Aspects that the learner has had difficulty with should be discussed honestly. Was it the method or style of instruction or coaching that caused problems? Were the targets for achievement set too high? Was the learner trying enough or too hard? Were there sufficient chances to practise before starting the activity? By breaking down what may appear to the learner to be an insurmountable and complex problem, each part can be simplified and dealt with separately. It is also worth noting that Coaches, Mentors and Assessors will find the process stimulating and helpful in their own development, in fact to describe these situations merely as 'two-way processes' is almost to understate the case.

How would it feel to you?

A useful way to begin to understand how to give appropriate feedback, in content, style and tone, is to consider how you feel when you ask for or receive feedback yourself. Ask yourself, when receiving feedback from another person, do you . . .

- listen actively to their description of your behaviour or performance?
- carefully consider what is being said, trying to see the situation from their point of view?
- weigh up the pros and cons of changing or modifying your behaviour?
- enter into a calm discussion about your views on their comments?
- mutually agree upon subsequent action?
- ask for any support or help you think will be necessary?
- thank them for their feedback?

Be honest. There are probably as many 'No' answers as 'Yes' ones. By reversing the role it is easy therefore to see some of the difficulties facing a recipient of feedback; we may:

- be afraid of what others think of us;
- wonder about the motives behind the feedback. Is it honest? Can they be trusted?

- fear a loss of face or independence even if we do recognise the need for help;
- lose confidence and feel inferior.

If Coaches, Mentors and Assessors are sensitive to these issues and constantly remind themselves by 'looking in the mirror', they will avoid the pitfalls of insensitive and inappropriate feedback.

It may be all too easy for the Coach, Mentor and Assessor to take the relationship aspect of their roles for granted, particularly if a Coach and Mentor have been working with their learner or protégé for some time. In the work situation issues of power and authority often underlie working relationships. And the learner or protégé usually understands only too well that they are often in a dependent and somewhat subordinate role *vis-à-vis* their Coach and Mentor. It is not always easy therefore to create a relaxed, informal and supporting relationship. This is particularly true if the culture of the organisation is bureaucratic or aggressively hierarchical and results oriented. Recognising the reality of the organisational culture pressures is important. It will help both parties to develop realistic expectations. It is important also to appreciate the effects that differences in age, sex, educational background and different cultures can have. This is not to say that they are necessarily obstacles but simply to point out that lack of awareness and sensitivity of the issues may make feedback sessions strained and demotivating.

Visualising successful performance

An extremely powerful way of increasing motivation and enhancing the will to succeed is to teach the learner how to visualise themselves performing an activity successfully and smoothly. Before attempting the task, encourage them to use their mind's eye and project themselves forward in time to see themselves doing the task well. Sportsmen and women often use this technique and visualise themselves carrying out each action in slow motion. They concentrate on mentally rehearsing each step and then grooming it until it is perfect. Whenever the action is unclear or hazy, they re-run this mental video until a perfect sequence is logged in their memory bank. This allows them to relax when they actually perform and rely on their memory to steer them to a successful result. In a business context, this technique can be adapted to help, for example, a nervous presenter. Getting the presenter to see themselves up there talking fluently to the audience, hearing their words putting across a point persuasively, seeing their gestures adding emphasis and their amusing anecdote drawing smiles and appreciation from the audience, all help build up confidence that they will be successful.

Harnessing the essential mental qualities

Building confidence then is about harnessing the mind of the learner. In Tim Gallwey's book, *The Inner Game of Tennis*, he talks about the two Selfs that are part of a performer's character. Self 1 is the 'teller' who instructs, evaluates and tries to control the performance. Self 2 is the 'doer' who actually performs the task, often unconsciously and automatically. In Tim's sporting analogies, you can often see and hear the two Selfs having a conversation! Self 1 is usually exhorting Self 2 to try harder and do specific things, as well as criticising what is happening. This can get in the way of Self 2's natural flow and abilities by creating a 'busy mind' and distracting the performance.

For the learner, the danger is that they try too hard and complicate and confuse themselves with too many of their own instructions. Poor results then encourage self-doubt to creep in which can begin a downward spiral. The secret is for Self 1 to trust its other half and simply let it perform. Self 1 demands a role, however, so the learner must programme it with images of the task and of performing it successfully. Holding back on criticism and replacing this only with observation allows Self 2 to make subtle adjustments and perform better.

John Whitmore, in his book *The Winning Mind*, takes this process further. He has developed a list of essential mental qualities to help the learner:

- Responsibility: taking personal responsibility for both successes and failures and not blaming other factors. Responsibility empowers the learner to take action, not wallow about in recriminations.
- Awareness: is most simply described as focussing on what is going on around you whilst performing. Being conscious of all factors in the environment and in the body allows the learner to self-correct their actions.
- Concentration: this involves remaining in a passive state while focussed on the task but remaining receptive to ideas and

thoughts. By not trying too hard the learner avoids the anxiety and pressure on themselves.

- Relaxation: is about containing Self 1 by keeping the chatter and instructions to a minimum. When the learner lets concerns about the future or regrets about the past into their mind they also let in anxiousness.
- Detachment: involves the learner in standing apart mentally from the activity and observing their actions. Maintaining a free and flexible state keeps Self 1 at bay.
- Commitment: this aspect encapsulates the will to win in three steps. First, the goal must be achievable to the learner, second, obstacles to achievement must be eliminated and, finally, the will must be supported by 100 per cent of honest effort.
- Trust: by being fully prepared the learner can trust their own mind and body to reproduce the action or task. Self 2 takes over the driving seat and lets Self 1 merely observe how well the performer has done - without judgement.

These concepts, although relatively easy to explain, are really quite sophisticated to apply and require careful study and practice. But they are important ideas to master and employ.

A final tip for the learner which John Whitmore advocates is to find a personal stimulus that creates a positive and relaxed mind and use it either as an outlet before performing or even during the activity. Examples might include listening to a favourite piece of music on a personal stereo or recalling a poem that inspires them. Physical activity, such as a visit to the gym or a short run, can have a relaxing effect too. All of these techniques Whitmore believes help people to understand and capture the essential qualities of the mind and support a confident and positive approach by the learner.

Handling the feedback session

There are a range of ideas and techniques which can be used to build confidence and the will to succeed but usually they have to be employed in one-to-one situations. How the feedback is handled on a day-to-day basis is therefore crucial.

It is important to try always to balance the necessity for giving negative messages with positive ones wherever possible. Strengths should be balanced with weaknesses and the aim should be to be fair as well as totally honest. It also helps to keep feedback as immediate as possible. The question of timing is crucial, particularly if the session is likely to be disappointing – don't delay it. And don't give feedback in small amounts. You needn't mention every single fault but you should concentrate mainly on the essentials. If you start with 'picky' small points you may create an atmosphere that makes discussion of more important topics unnecessarily difficult.

If you are asked for your advice you should give it. But remember some of us like to give advice because it makes us feel important. Sometimes this only serves to satisfy our ego. Wherever possible, the request for advice should be deflected into a question which encourages the learners to work the solutions out for themselves. Similarly you should avoid trying to persuade or even argue. If the other person becomes defensive or obstructive, try to discover the reason for this reaction and build on that towards a positive action.

Be aware that over praising is often dangerous as it can confuse the situation. Being supportive does not mean constant praising. It means creating an atmosphere in which the learner, protégé or candidate can admit faults or fears, knowing they will be understood if not necessarily endorsed. Always strive to be sensitive to the other person and avoid unwittingly denying the individual their feelings with hasty comments like 'you don't mean that' or 'you have no reason to feel that way'. It helps too if you can keep your comments as descriptive as possible and avoid making value judgements or giving the appearance of making a personal attack. Avoid saying 'what a stupid way to do it'; try rather 'that was not necessarily the best way to do it'. Some tips are easier to give than to apply, but they will all produce a positive response.

Assessors involved in a qualification process have some particular issues to address. They need to be able to describe the meaning of results, particularly test scores, in a way that correctly reflects their implications but which is also intelligible to the candidate. And they have to be able to make suggestions as to what the candidate can and should do next in order to reach competence. Clearly this will need careful handling if the candidate has just been told that the assessment of their current performance is not yet able to be judged as competent.

All the skills I have discussed in the other chapters are important in handling feedback. It is equally important to recognise that other behaviours have the potential to destroy the value of feedback sessions. For instance:

- being quick to disagree or even argue;
- being overly critical;

- being distant or aloof;
- interrupting repeatedly;
- ignoring comments, ideas, feelings;
- not asking any questions at all;
- appearing to be in a hurry to finish the session.

Making winners

Giving feedback which builds confidence and success is not simple. Done effectively, feedback is about the making of winners. But remember it is fundamentally a two-way process. When in doubt try to put yourself in the recipient's place or, to quote the proverb, 'Do unto others as you would be done by'.

The following checklist should help you apply the essentials of giving effective feedback.

Checklist

1. You get more out of people if you are sensitive to their situation and treat them as adults.
2. Imagine how you would feel if you were on the receiving end.
3. Feedback should be honest but also fair.
4. Balance both negative and positive messages.
5. Don't avoid weaknesses but always balance them by emphasising strengths as well.
6. Choose the appropriate tone and language.
7. Aim for clarity and, where criticism is needed, keep it simple and constructive.
8. Encourage people to take responsibility for their own development.
9. Be well organised yourself and hold regular progress reviews.
10. Read Tim Gallwey's and John Whitmore's books to help develop a positive and winning attitude.

APPENDIX 1
Some Useful References and Additional Reading

How do adults learn?

T. Buzan (1984), *Use Your Head*, Ariel Books/BBC Books (paperback,revised).

K. P. Cross (1986), *Adults as Learners*, Jossey-Bass, San Francisco.

P. Honey and A. Mumford (1986), *Using Your Learning Styles* (2nd edn, UK), Peter Honey.

D. A. Kolb and R. Fry (1975), *Towards an Applied Theory of Experiential Learning*, McBer and Co, Boston.

How do people become qualified?

M. Bees and M. Swords (1990), *National Vocational Qualifications and Further Education*, Kogan Page and NCVQ, London.

J. W. Burke (Ed) (1989), *Competency Based Education and Training*, Falmer Press, London.

G. Jessup (1991), *Outcomes: NVQs and the Emerging Model of Education and Training*, Falmer Press, London.

NCVQ (1989), *Guide to National Vocational Qualifications*.

What is evidence of competence?

City and Guilds Handbook (1991), City and Guilds of London Institute.

CNAA (1990), *The Assessment of Management Competencies*, Council for National Academic Awards.

MCI (1991), *Guidelines for Action*, Management Charter Initiative.

NCVQ (1991), *The NVQ Framework*, National Council for Vocational Qualifications.

RSA (1991), *A Guide to all RSA Schemes*, Royal Society of Arts.

What do I have to do if I am a Coach?

R. Buckley and J. Caple (1991), *One-to-one Training and Coaching Skills*, Kogan Page, London.

T. Gallwey (1974), *The Inner Game of Tennis*, Random House, New York.

D. Hemery (1986), *The Pursuit of Sporting Excellence*: A Study of Sport's Highest Achievers, Willow Books, London.

D. Megginson and T. Baydell (1979), *A Manager's Guide to Coaching*, British Association for Commercial and Industrial Education, London.

What do I have to do if I am a Mentor?

D. Clutterbuck (1991), *Everyone Needs a Mentor* (2nd edn), Institute of Personnel Management.

E. M. Goldratt & J. Cox (1989), *The Goal*, Gower, Aldershot.

The Institution of Industrial Managers (1991), *Manual of Good Practice*, The IIM Leader Series, MCI.

T. J. Peters and R. H. Waterman (1982), *In Search of Excellence*, Harper and Row, New York.

What do I have to do if I am an Assessor?

S. Fletcher (1991), *NVQs, Standards and Competence*, Kogan Page, London.

S. Fletcher (1992), *Competence Based Assessment Techniques*, Kogan Page, London.

P. Iles and M. Blanksby (1991), *Assessing Skills at Work*, Kogan Page, London.

Institute of Personnel Managers (1989), Fact Sheet Series No. 22, October, IPM.

S. Simosko (1991), *APL: A Practical Guide for Professionals*, Kogan Page, London.

How can I listen and observe more efficiently?

D. Bone (1988), *A Practical Guide to Effective Listening*, Kogan Page, London.

D. Mackenzie Davey (1989), *How to be a Good Judge of Character*, Kogan Page, London.

D. Morris (1977), *Man Watching: A Field Guide to Human Behaviour*, Cape, London.

A. Pease (1984), *Body Language*, Sheldon Press, London.

How can I ask the right question?

G. Wells (1978), *How to Communicate*, McGraw Hill, London.

J. Whitmore (1987), *The Winning Mind*, Fernhurst Books, Hove.

How can I give feedback which builds confidence and success?

Elwood N. Chapman (1988), *How to Develop a Positive Attitude*, Kogan Page, London.

T. Gallwey (1974), *The Inner Game of Tennis*, Random House, New York.

J. Whitmore (1987), *The Winning Mind*, Fernhurst Books, Hove.

How can I set goals to develop competence?

R. Mager (1991), *Goal Analysis*, Kogan Page, London.

APPENDIX 2
Edited Version of KPMG Peat Marwick Career Planner

This is a good example of a self-assessment guide which was referred to in Chapter 6. The following edited extracts illustrated the scope of the document:

At KPMG Peat Marwick our aim is to help you with your career development as much as we can and this career planner is part of that assistance. It has been designed to assist you in planning and monitoring your personal development and, in particular, to:

- identify your strengths and weaknesses;
- consider your goals and the skills you need;
- create practical action plans, including training, to achieve your career development goals;
- identify those areas within the firm you would most like to explore;
- provide a basis for discussion with your counsellor.

How to use the career planner

The career planner is designed to provide a five-year rolling record of your personal development. It can, of course, continue to be used beyond that point and we would encourage you to do so – clearly your personal development will continue throughout your career. As a student, you should use the career planner every six months in preparation for regular counselling interviews, although you may also find it useful for reference at other times. After qualification, the planner is designed to be used annually, although this is not intended to be restrictive and you should use it to suit your needs. You should fill in the section of the planner that reflects your current grade within the firm.

The planner is your personal record. Your counsellor will not ask to see it, but he or she will want to ensure that you have completed the questions and prepared for the interview.

The structure of the career planner

The planner contains a series of questions organised under four main headings:

- Where am I now and how have I progressed?
- How do I want to develop?
- What opportunities are available?
- How could I get there?

These are the four phases of career development and should all be considered each time you review your progress.

Preparing for your counselling interview

The final question asks you to consider the key issues you would like to raise at your next counselling interview. You should, therefore, complete the self-assessment questions several days beforehand. You should identify the important issues and consider how to address them with your counsellor.

Your counsellor will discuss these issues with you and, where appropriate, your senior manager, to help you formulate constructive action plans wherever possible. As a firm we are committed to helping you achieve your goals, but your needs have to be balanced with ours and those of our clients. The counselling process is designed to establish wherever possible, how that balance can be achieved.

Where am I now and how have I progressed?

Question 1: *What technical skills have I acquired or improved on in the last six months or since last reviewing my career?*

Question 2: *What non-technical skills have I acquired or improved on in the last six months or since last reviewing my career?*

Question 3: *What other qualifications do I have? What else have I achieved in my life over the last six months or since last reviewing my career?* (Think more broadly about other areas of your life outside KPMG Peat Marwick. You may have attended evening courses or chaired a group or professional body and in so doing acquired interpersonal skills which may contribute to your career development. Activities such as buying or selling your own property can also help develop useful organisation and management skills.)

Question 4: *What type of assignments do I find most satisfying and which least satisfying, and why? Am I getting as much as possible out of these assignments?*

Question 5: *Under what conditions do I work most effectively, and under what conditions least effectively, and why?*

Question 6: *Overall, have I found my work satisfying and have I developed over the last six months or since last reviewing my career? Why, or why not?* (Consider the wide variety of work experience you have had over the past six months. Try to assess the balance between enjoyment and development and how they both contribute to job satisfaction.)

Question 7: *What have I learned about the services the firm provides over the last six months or since last reviewing my career?*

Question 8: *Year 1, first six months: Is KPMG Peat Marwick living up to my original expectations? Year 1, second six months and after: Have I achieved my previous goals?*

How do I want to develop?

The second set of questions (9–11) is designed to help you assess your future career development – in particular to help you create achievable career goals. Goal setting is a key element in career development. It provides you with a focus, a statement of ambitions and aspirations, and a target to achieve. It is important that your goals are realistic within the time available; otherwise they will not represent achievable targets. A continual process of realistic goal setting will ensure that you develop a truly satisfying career.

Question 9: *What skills or knowledge could I improve for my present work?*

Question 10: *What are my work goals for the next six to twelve months? For the next two to three years?* (These goals should be practical and achievable within the set period. They will vary with experience. Look at your list of skills and goals and draw up a work plan for the next year to see how and when you can achieve them. Consider any obstacles and how these may be overcome. Think, too, about how your short-term goals should reflect your long-term goals. For example, if your aim is to become a financial executive, consider how you might enhance your management skills.)

Question 11: *What are my priorities outside work for the next six to twelve months? Do these have an impact on my career?*

Question 12: *What opportunities are available within the firm to prepare me for my future career?*

Question 13: *What knowledge do I need to acquire?* (Consider what further knowledge you need before achieving your goals and the extent to which you can gain this within general practice or a specialist role. Think specifically about the need to develop industry-related knowledge in, for example, banking and finance. Consider the difference between a knowledge base and the technical and non-technical skills which are the tools of the trade and which enable you to use your knowledge and work effectively.)

Question 14: *What technical skills do I need to develop or improve?*

Question 15: *What non-technical skills do I need to develop or improve?*

Question 16: *What action do I need to take to pursue my career development? What assistance do I require from others?* (Look back through all of the above questions. The aim of this question is to help you focus on the key issues and see what you need to do next to develop your career. Now outline a realistic career development plan setting out your goals in detail for the next six to twelve months and, more broadly, for the next two to three years and how you propose to achieve them. Your ability to do this will increase as you become more experienced and able to determine what you find satisfying.)

Question 17: *What are the key issues I would like to raise in my next counselling meeting?* (There may be a number of unresolved issues following your self-assessment. There will also be areas you have identified where you need further training or practical experience. Highlight all of these in preparation for your counselling meeting. Look back at the action points arising from your last counselling meeting to see whether they have been progressed or, if not, whether they are of continuing relevance to your career development plan.)

Career development and your future

We hope that this career planner helps you to clarify what you have achieved to date, your short- and long-term career goals and the training and experience you will need in order to achieve them. Career planning and development is an ongoing process, and personal commitment is essential to its success.

APPENDIX 3
Edited Version of ICI Pharmaceuticals Performance Review Document

This is an example of the 'open-ended' approach to assessing against performance standards, discussed in Chapter 6.

Stage 1 – business role

Manager to ensure that the job holder has a clear, up-to-date documented statement of his/her business role.

Stage 2 – performance planning

Develop joint commitment between you and your manager to achieve targets which are derived from and contribute to your business role.

- Are they SMART?
- Are all job evaluation accountabilities covered?
- Can/how does this develop you?

Stage 3 – performance development

Define skills/knowledge/experience needed and agree coaching plan to achieve agreed targets.

- Can this be coached?
- Who should coach it?
- What formal training is required?

FIG A3.1 ICI PHARMACEUTICAL MODEL

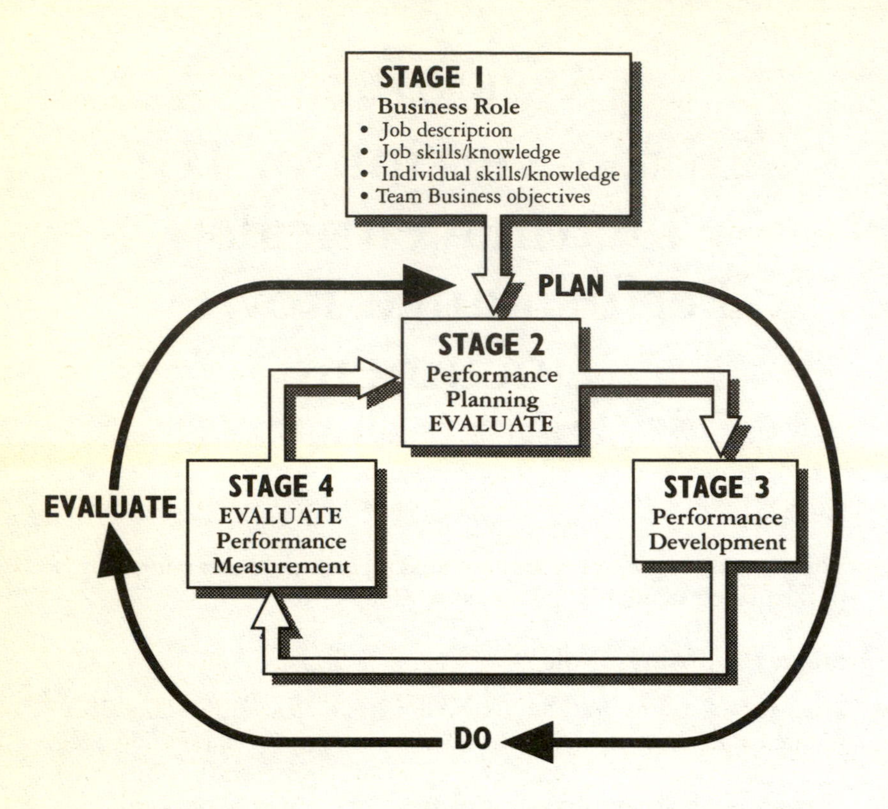

Stage 4 – performance measurement

a) Monitor achievement vs targets to provide ongoing feedback to Stage 2.
b) Derive an annual assessment of performance which will contribute to the determination/recognition of reward and your future development.
   - Have you obtained feedback?
   - Qualities/quantities?
   - Have circumstances changed?

In discussing and agreeing your targets, individual development plan and achievement, consider:

Performance planning and measurement

Target

- Are all aspects of your business covered appropriately?
- Is there balance between maintaining standards and enhancing your performance?
- Establish and agree relative priorities.
- Are the measurable success criteria clear – how will your performance be measured quantitatively or qualitatively?

Check – is it

• Specific	– unambiguous, concrete?
• Measurable	– how many, how much, specified action, success indicators – are these really measurable?
• Achievable	– challenging but do-able, not soft or over-optimistic?
• Relevant	– to your job or your team's business objectives?
• Timed	– are the milestone/completion dates clear?
Discussion date	– when was the target set?
Review dates	– at least quarterly although short-term targets will require earlier review.
Progress Notes	– use this space to cover key points/notes (eg changing priorities, progress, actions) discussed at review meetings which will contribute to the final measurement of performance against this target.
Target Achievement	– was the target met? Over- or under-achieved?
Comments	– on level of achievement; – any relevant additional information on performance, eg how you achieved this target.

Individual development plan

Knowledge/Skill Area	– which is it? What is it?
SMART goal	– what is it that you will do better/differently? Is it SMART?

Development	– how will you develop this skill?
Activities	– knowledge? Coaching, training, other? Be specific.
Review dates	– when would it be sensible and relevant to review your progress?
Progress/Comment	– have you achieved what was wanted? If so, what helped/hindered? What needs to be done now?

Performance summary

Overall Assessment

- How has your performance improved during the year, and what contribution has this made to overall business performance?
- Other significant activities which have not been reflected in your targets.
- Which targets were met, over/under achieved?
- What priority did they have?
- Were some met at the cost of others? Was the overall balance right?
- Were there any other factors which added to/detracted from the overall level of performance (eg reorganisation, changed responsibilities/accountabilities, work or non-work related stress, additional resources etc.)?
- What progress has been made towards achieving development goals? Has this been reflected in performance?

APPENDIX 4
Edited Version of Philips Components Performance Review Document

This is an example of the 'structured' approach to assessing against performance standards, discussed in Chapter 6.

The Performance Review procedures have been revised by a Working Party in order to underline the changes in our culture that we believe are needed at this time. In addition to enabling each employee to see more clearly what the company expects of him/her, the revised processes emphasise the need for each employee to:

- Aim for stretching targets
- Accept necessary changes
- Take risks where appropriate
- Improve requisite organisational skills

The new procedures provide *benefits* for all concerned.

Performance review

The Performance Review meeting is attended by the Employee and Manager only. The Performance Review includes discussion of:

- Performance against Principal Accountabilities;
- Performance against previously agreed targets and agreed new targets;

- The extent to which the employee has kept his/her promises;
- The extent to which he/she has met agreed deadlines;
- The quality of the employee's work;
- A personal profile of *how* the job is carried out;
- Actions by the manager which are needed to assist the employee to achieve the targets in the coming period;
- Development and training needs and plans.

The discussion is recorded during the meeting on the Performance Review Form, a copy of which is attached. A copy of the completed Form is given to the Employee after it has been seen by his or her Manager's manager. Detailed guidance is given in the attached notes.

Detailed guidelines

Before giving a blank copy of a Performance Review Form to the employee, the Manager should:

- Complete all parts of Page 1
- Enter the 'Targets for Last Period' on Page 2

Both Manager and Employee should then *prepare* for the Review discussion by separately completing as much as possible of the Form – ie entering the ratings etc as each sees them. This preparation by both is an essential part of the process: the Employee should be given adequate time to prepare. A copy of the job description should be available.

At the Review discussion both drafts should be tabled and the entries compared section by section. The entries on the final version of the Performance Review Form should be agreed jointly by Manager and Employee – if necessary, differences of opinion may be recorded. If the Employee wishes, he/she will be given a copy of the completed Performance Review Form at the end of the discussion, but a copy will in any case be provided after the Manager's manager has seen it.

Principal accountabilities

The Ratings for Principal Accountabilities are:

Excellent – Exceeds all requirements.
Performance at this level is rare but possible.

Very good – Meets requirements but definitely exceeds in some respects.

Good - Meets the requirements.
This is what most employees would expect to be.
Fair - Does not meet some of the requirements.
Poor - Fails to meet the requirements.
Little contribution is made.

Targets

General notes on target setting

Targets must be agreed between the Manager and the subordinate. The target should be specified in such a way that it will be clear when it is met and must include a time-frame in which it should be achieved.

The maximum number of targets allowed is four but fewer than four may be set provided they form an adequately demanding goal. Targets may be 'multiple targets' in some cases eg 'Complete all 90 day objectives within the correct period' or 'Maintain all achieved levels of targets set last period'.

Performance against promises and deadlines

Indicate in this section how the subordinate performs against *their own* promises and deadlines. In some areas, deadlines may be structured eg reports to be submitted by a certain date each month. In other areas, promises may be more appropriate eg to respond to customers. Although the emphasis will vary, it is important that the performance against commitment is assessed.

Personal profile in the job

The objective is to provide an opportunity for the Jobholder and Manager to discuss the strengths which the individual brings to the job and examine the weaknesses which may require attention. The aim is improved performance and development of the individual. The page is divided into three parts:

1. A relevance to the job column.
2. A comments section.
3. The profile characteristics.

Relevance to the job

Rate how relevant this characteristic is in the current job. Use High (H), Medium (M), Low (L) or Not Applicable (N/A). Sections rated Not Applicable should not be assessed, all other sections must be assessed.

The comments section

Discussion would obviously be concentrated towards characteristics with a high relevance but with a less than desirable performance and it is anticipated that these would be further elaborated within the comments section. This would highlight a particular training or development need.

The profile characteristics

The purpose of this part is to focus attention on particular skills and attitudes, and only those elements which are needed in the job should be assessed. The objective is to understand performance in the current job, not to examine potential.

It is recognised that it is not easy to categorise people into boxes but all applicable sections must be assessed. Where there is difficulty in finding an exact fit, tick the box with the closest fit, or if necessary, tick two boxes (but no more than two) and make an explanatory note in the comments section. There is space available on the back page to make further comments or to cover topics not included on this page.

The following is a brief outline of the topics (Competences) covered.

Job knowledge
This relates to know-how required to do the job and may for example cover product knowledge, accounting, marketing, sales and systems skills. The know-how could be gained on the job or by external qualifications/experience.

Vision/creativity
To what extent does the Jobholder consider and come up with imaginative and realistic ideas as opposed to only considering day-to-day issues.

Planning of work
This is an indication of the skills which the individual brings to the organisation of work to meet priorities and objectives.

Risk taking
This covers the approach the person adopts to challenging and uncertain situations, together with the success achieved if and when risks are taken.

Approach to change/flexibility
This is largely a question of attitude. Is there a positive approach to change - actively seeking it, a passive approach - willing to accept it, or a negative approach - resisting it?

Problem solving
Are problems tackled eagerly, imaginatively and successfully or are they avoided? Success in dealing with problems should be judged by whether or not they recur (ie continuous 'fire fighting' may indicate a less effective approach).

Decision making
What is the Jobholder's approach to decision making? Are decisions made readily, with clarity and correctness, or is it difficult to get decisions made?

Delegation and control
This refers to the management of subordinates and considers the delegation and control/monitoring skills of the Manager.

Initiative and drive
What attitude does the person bring to the job, eg self-motivation and the ability to make the most of opportunities or attitudes which indicates a less ambitious person? How persistent is the Jobholder in tackling tasks?

Ability to work under pressure
This is an indication of the extent to which the Jobholder copes with pressure from all causes.

Communication and listening
This considers the Jobholder's approach to communicating with all persons with whom they come into contact and the skills which they bring to communicating, eg clarity, brevity, etc.

Persuasiveness
This assesses the skill and attitude which the Jobholder brings to convincing others (subordinates, bosses, offline etc) to adopt a particular course of action.

Team working
This reviews the contribution which the Jobholder makes in team/group situations. It relates also to some extent to an attitude to working within a team. Really effective team members are not necessarily those who dominate the group.

Development of staff
Does the Jobholder take an active and positive interest in developing staff for future needs or is this one of the aspects to which less than adequate attention is paid?

Leadership
To what extent are leadership skills shown? Does the Jobholder lead others well or badly or is leadership avoided? This skill may apply to all staff and not just those formally appointed to supervisory or management positions.

Development and training issues

In addition to discussing the Training Plan for the Employee for the coming year, consideration should be given to possible career development matters – eg experience that may be needed in preparation for possible future jobs.

Employee's comments

For Employee to add comments if wished. These should be written by the Employee at the review meeting.

Overall view of performance

This is the Manager's view of performance. Performance Assessment is clearly influenced by the immediate Manager's view, but it is not the only input. Discussion at senior level is needed to ensure that consistent standards are applied across the company.

Signatures

The Manager and Employee should sign the Form at the end of the discussion. Other appropriate signatures - Manager's manager and any functional manager - should be obtained as soon as possible afterwards.

Distribution

The Manager should then give a copy of the completed Form to the Employee and send a copy to Personnel.

APPENDIX 5
Mentoring Policy Statement from Personnel Division ICI Pharmaceuticals

The Mentor concept

When looking for a model of good practice of induction within Personnel Department, it is evident how important the role of Mentor support is. In discussion with members of Personnel Department there is a consensus opinion in favour of Mentor support during induction, both by people who have received Mentor support and others who have not.

The role of Mentor and how it should be carried out

The new member of the Department will be learning continuously and a key element of the Mentor's job will be to help guide that learning process by challenging, checking and consolidating - learning is improved by a positive environment.

The Mentor should highlight any areas of concern to the individual with the progress of the induction process.

The Mentor and individual should meet frequently for short periods of time rather than infrequently and for longer periods. A practical example of this would be to arrange a meeting once a week initially, extending to once a fortnight at a later date.

The Mentor will be helping the individual learn more about the induction process and its significance, challenging any conclusions which may have been reached.

Selecting the Mentor

A Mentor must be appointed before the individual joins the Department and the concept of mentoring should be clearly explained to them by the manager.

Attempt to identify the individual's potential training needs and assign a Mentor who may have the skills to help in this area:

- Look for a similarity between either the jobs of the individual and the Mentor or of problems experienced/anticipated.
- The Mentor must be clear about the jobs and of the importance of the role being carried out by him/her.
- The Mentor must be able to counsel correctly (it may be necessary for him/her to attend a Counselling Skills Course, if applicable).
- The Mentor should not be involved in the design or formulation of the induction programme (however, he/she may be participative in the actual training given to the individual).

The Mentor needs to be well equipped using training sessions and coaching in order to carry out the role successfully. Mentors may wish to meet periodically to exchange views, compare standards and approach, and discuss any problems with which they have been faced and agree actions resulting.

A mentor is a 'wise counsellor'.

There will be times when the Mentor may find conflict between their role and that of the line-manager within the Personnel function. Where business requirements are paramount, the role of the Mentor is explicit. These prerequisites are:

- experience in ICI employment;
- an interest in training;
- an interest in development of colleagues;
- an interest in the management of people;
- the ability to challenge ideas;
- be open to new ideas.

As well as being receptive to new ideas and open to change, a Mentor must also be positively critical and challenging. A job advert has been drawn up and included in this section to highlight the attributes needed by someone assuming a Mentor support role.

The Mentor must not be the manager of the individual because the roles may become confused.

The relationship

It is vital to the success of mentoring that the Mentor and the individual have an open relationship with *confidentiality* being the most essential factor. Trust, rapport and mutual respect for each other should also be in evidence. The mentor should be used as a 'sounding board' by the individual when trying to solve their problems and difficulties. It is not the Mentor's role to speak directly to the manager unless agreement is reached.

Benefits and conclusions

As an organisation, we should be concerned with the effective development of people and the Mentor scheme enables this to be undertaken positively for people who may exercise influence in the future.

The mentoring concept should be under regular evaluation and review by the Department's managers, the Mentors and new employees.

APPENDIX 6
Sample NVQ Performance Standard

This is an extract from the MCI Standards of Management Competence showing the breakdown of a single Element.

Element 9.1 *Lead meetings and group discussions to solve problems and make decisions.*

Performance criteria

a) A suitable number of people appropriate to the context and purpose of the meeting are invited and attend.
b) The purpose of the meeting is clearly established with other group members at the outset.
c) Information and summaries are presented clearly, at an appropriate time.
d) Style of leadership helps group members to contribute fully.
e) Unhelpful arguments and digressions are effectively discouraged.
f) Any decisions taken fall within the group's authority.
g) Decisions are recorded accurately and passed on as necessary to the appropriate people.

Range indicators

Meetings and group discussion led by the manager involve:

- discussion of alternatives;
- group decision-making;
- consultation.

Problems analysed are to do with operations with the manager's line responsibility. Meetings are informal and usually characterised by the lack of detailed minutes, rules of procedure or standing orders. Those present at the meetings/discussions are other members of the manager's team.

Source of evidence
Performance in the workplace in differing types of meetings over time. Questioning may be required to elucidate rationale for approach taken in leading each kind of meeting.

Forms of evidence
Direct observation, supported by documentation, eg minutes, action notes, etc, as appropriate, Personal Report and extensive witness testimony.

Index